Laying The Foundations

A history and archaeology
of the Trent Valley
sand and gravel industry

By Tim Cooper

CBA Research Report 159
Council for British Archaeology 2008

Published in 2008 by the Council for British Archaeology
St Mary's House, 66 Bootham, York YO30 7BZ
Copyright © 2008 Author and Council for British Archaeology
British Library Cataloguing in Publication Data
A catalogue record for this book is available from the British Library
ISBN 978-1-902771-76-2
Page design and typesetting by Carnegie Publishing Ltd
Printed and bound in the UK by the Alden Press, Oxford
The publisher acknowledges with gratitude a grant from English Heritage
towards the cost of publication

Front:
background Former gravel workings at Attenborough, now the site of the
Nature Reserve Visitor Centre (Tim Cooper/ARCUS)
foreground Ready-mixed concrete truck belonging to Trent Gravels Ltd of
Attenborough at an M1 construction site in the Midlands *c* 1965 (by courtesy
of Michael Arthur)

Back:
Reed beds at Attenborough Nature Reserve (by courtesy of Nottinghamshire
Wildlife Trust/David Eberlin)

Contents

List of Figures

Acknowledgements

The idea for this book was originally conceived by Jon Humble in his role as English Heritage Inspector of Monuments for the East Midlands Region, and was endorsed by the Trent Valley Geoarchaeology Group. A research project was then set up by ARCUS at the University of Sheffield, financed by the Aggregates Levy Sustainability Fund and administered by English Heritage, to which I became attached as research assistant. I very much welcomed the opportunity this provided to renew my long-standing working relationship with colleagues at ARCUS, in particular its director James Symonds, who acted as project manager, Anna Badcock who handled the financial administration, and Marcus Abbott who took care of the graphics.

The project benefited greatly from the knowledge and expertise of a number of people connected with the Trent Valley aggregates industry and quarrying in general. Ian Thomas, Director of the National Stone Centre, acted as a project consultant, providing valuable assistance in the early stages, allowing full access to the centre's library resources, and making detailed comments on an early draft of the book. Mike Arthur, former Technical Director of the Institute of Quarrying, shared his long experience of the industry, made a generous loan of materials relating to Trent Gravels Ltd and the ready-mixed concrete industry, and also commented on the first draft. For helping me get some feeling for sand and gravel quarries I am particularly grateful for the time given for site visits by Cemex (Mick Turner, Gary Pell and Mick Bugg at Attenborough), Hanson Aggregates (Bob Woodbridge at Shardlow) and Tarmac (Tom Dodsley at Hoveringham). In addition, Tom Dodsley, whose retirement from the industry coincided with the decommissioning of the historic Hoveringham Quarry, provided answers to the numerous technical questions that cropped up as I prepared the final draft of the book. Also within the industry I am grateful for generous assistance rendered, and material provided or lent, by Neil Beards (Tarmac), Tim Deal and David Atkinson (Lafarge).

One of the greatest debts owed by the project, and me personally, is to the people connected with the industry who answered my adverts in the press and agreed to be interviewed and, in a number of cases, to lend photographs and other materials in their possession. A full list of the interviewees will be found in Appendix One but I would like here to record my particular thanks to Dennis Thacker, Nigel Hunt, Terry Cliff and Bryan Atkin, all of whom lent important materials for my research. In addition, Dennis Thacker generously gave up working time to give me guided tours of the historic workings at Besthorpe, Girton and Winthorpe. Throughout the course of the project I was struck by the eagerness with which men and women connected to the industry wanted their story to be told, and the obvious affection in which they hold a line of work that generally attracts less than positive attention from the world at large. I can only hope that this book does them some justice.

It is with sadness that I must acknowledge the importance to this project of the late Mrs Carol Mellors who, by introducing me to her uncle, Durgin Thornhill, opened a window on the otherwise unknown early history of sand and gravel extraction in the Trent Valley. Together with Durgin, her father Frank Thornhill had been one of the pioneers of the industry, and it is to her memory that this book is dedicated.

TNC
Sheffield, June 2008

Author's Note

For much of the period with which this book is concerned, various imperial units of measurement were used. In order to avoid intrusive conversions in the text, the main examples and their metric equivalent are given below.

Gravel production and loads in tons: 1 ton = 1.01605 tonnes

Occasionally, in early days, hundredweights: 1 hundredweight = 50kg

Concrete output and production (and occasionally gravel output) in cubic yards: 1 cubic yard = 0.764555 cubic metres

Areas of quarry sites in acres: 1 acre = 0.4047 hectares

Gravel size and plant components in inches: 1 inch = 2.54cm

Before 1969 all the detailed data was in cubic yards (with average conversion factors given as footnotes in the output statistics), with the exception of the total county production figures before WWII which were in imperial tons. Before the implementation of the Factories Act, 1937, official statistics only covered mineral workings more than 20 feet (6.1m) deep, thus excluding many sand and gravel operations. This needs to be borne in mind when assessing the relative significance of the industry before this date. I am grateful to Ian Thomas of the National Stone Centre for information on this point.

In the early days of the industry, a sand and gravel working was commonly referred to as a 'pit' and though the term 'quarry' was later widely adopted, both continued in use side by side. In this book, 'quarry' is generally the preferred term.

Foreword

Today almost all new development in the UK is constructed either wholly or partly from the products of mineral extraction. Because current and future extraction has the capacity to have significant effects, both positive and negative, on the environment, today's UK minerals industry is highly regulated by planning law and policy. The legacy of past quarrying and mining can form an important part of what we call the historic environment, and authentic materials are needed for conservation work, for repairs to historic buildings and for maintaining local distinctiveness with new construction. Modern society has literally been built on and out of minerals.

'Aggregates' are defined as granular materials used in construction and may be naturally occurring (such as sand and gravel), manufactured or recycled. Surprising it may seem, but in many respects the aggregates industry could be regarded as *the* quintessential industry of the 20th century, although one not quite as celebrated as the endeavours that brought us the motor car, the silicon chip, space travel and nuclear fission, the more commonly cited icons of the last century. There is, however, perhaps no other indigenous UK industry, in sum, which has spanned the whole of the 20th century, which has remained in robust health for all of this period, and which through its operations and products has had such a profound impact on the places where we live, work and recreate.

About 0.35% of the area of the UK currently has planning permission for mineral development, including extraction sites, processing plants, minerals waste tips and landscaping schemes. Of this, around 0.12% is specifically associated with aggregates production. Since the 1980s and the scaling-down of UK coal production, aggregates extraction is the last heavy industry that occurs widely throughout the countryside. In 2006, 229 million tonnes of primary aggregates were used by the UK construction industry. In addition, another 26 million tonnes were used for a wide variety of industrial, environmental and agricultural operations.[1] Today the industry is a highly skilled and technically proficient operation that seeks daily to grapple with the big issues of sustainable development, the future supply of minerals, and the implications of climate change.

But what is the story of the aggregates industry? How has it developed over time? How has it responded to and been shaped by the complex mix of influences, demands, and aspirations within society? What are the lessons of the past that might be relevant to the present and future of the industry? By comparison with some other forms of mineral extraction – such as the winning and working of metal ores, coal and dimensional stone – the origins and contribution of the aggregates industry are probably less widely recognised and certainly less well appreciated. This book, which contains Tim Cooper's ground-breaking research into the sand and gravel industry of the Trent Valley in central England, a seminal and pivotal region in the development of the industry, addresses these questions. It also makes, in the process, an important contribution towards redressing the imbalances in the ways in which the sand and gravel industry is perceived.

The research, writing and publication of this book has been funded by a grant from the Aggregates Levy Sustainability Fund (ALSF). The Aggregates Levy, which generates the ALSF, was introduced in 2002 by the UK government at the rate of £1.60 per tonne on all primary aggregates extraction. English Heritage distributes the historic environment funding stream of the ALSF on behalf of the Department for Environment, Food and Rural Affairs. It is therefore highly appropriate that this book has been enabled by the very activity that it sets out to examine. It is the first in-depth regional study of the UK sand and gravel industry, and as such it will be of interest to workers in the industry itself, people and communities who live and work in the Trent Valley, archaeologists, planners, and the many organisations that engage with and influence the shaping and management of our landscapes. It is a highly readable account of the industry that will appeal to both popular and academic audiences. Of particular note is the role in this book of the people who have worked in the industry – their conversations with the author are here repeated and this 'oral testimony' serves to bring the subject matter vividly to life. In this book, people are quite rightly centre-stage – they are not second-class citizens to plant, machinery and working methods – which, nevertheless, are also considered in due and rigorous detail.

Throughout the 20th century, many of England's river terraces have been exploited for their sand and gravel deposits, yet these were often also the areas that were favoured in the past for settlement, agriculture and burial. This is particularly true of the Trent Valley, the river having been a vital transport route, an economic lifeline and a geopolitical dividing line for thousands of years. Extraction of its sands and gravels has provided many opportunities for archaeological investigations, and the results of this work have transformed our understanding of the valley's historic and prehistoric past. Like minerals, archaeological remains are a finite and non-renewable resource – once lost or damaged, they cannot be re-created.

Just what constitutes England's heritage and what should be conserved for future generations is sometimes hotly debated – and, of course, views will change as society applies different values and different value systems to what it considers to be important, significant and relevant. Refreshingly, the views of individuals do not and will not always coincide with those of society. There can be no doubt, however, that the modern era is a legitimate period for study. By definition, today's landscapes will become tomorrow's heritage – therefore we have choice and the potential to influence what will become tomorrow's heritage more so for the modern era than for any other period in our past. In 2007 the UK Government became a signatory to the European Landscape Convention, which includes the creation of new landscapes as one of its key objectives. Rather than 'fossilising' our landscapes or turning them into a 'living museum', it is entirely logical that change may be the preferred choice of archaeologists as the very essence of what they study.

Few industries have the capacity to make a more significant contribution to our future landscapes than the sand and gravel industry. It is therefore essential that we work towards a better understanding of the past, current and future aims and objectives of the industry – and also that the industry has a clearer, reciprocal understanding of the aspirations and methods of archaeologists and the historic environment sector. This book offers an important contribution towards such an agenda for the future.

Jon Humble

Senior Policy Adviser (Minerals) & Inspector of Ancient Monuments

English Heritage

Notes

1 Quarry Products Association 2007.

≈ ONE ≈

History

The Trent and its region

The river Trent is not the longest river in Britain but, forming as it does a natural physical divide between the uplands of the north and west of England and the lowlands of the south and east, it is one of the most significant. At 275km from its rising in the Staffordshire moorlands to its eventual confluence with the Humber estuary, it is the third-longest river in England after the Thames and the Severn. Along that course it is joined by no fewer than 42 main tributaries; only the Severn carries a greater volume of water. Accounting for the drainage of some 20,000 km², or a little under 10% of the surface area of England, it passes through five counties and 23 separate units of local government, an area containing over 1,000 scheduled monuments and about the same number of conservation areas. More than four million people live in its main urban centres of Stoke, Derby, Nottingham, Burton and Newark, which together cover just over 10% of its land area, and in total about six million people live in the catchment area of the Trent (Fig 1). Over half of this region is agricultural.

By the beginning of the 21st century, the production of aggregate minerals, which includes sand, gravel and crushed rock, was the largest extractive industry in the UK, with over 200 million tonnes being produced each year. With an annual output of over 50 million tonnes, the Trent Valley region competed directly with the Thames Valley as the largest producer of aggregate minerals in England.[1] Some 10 million tonnes of this was in the form of sand and gravel, of which the Trent Valley was the most significant area of production outside the south-east of England (Fig 2).

Geology of Trent Valley sand and gravel

Depending on their age and geological origin, sand and gravel resources can be divided into bedrock or 'solid' deposits and superficial or 'drift' deposits. In the Trent Valley region, the bedrock deposits comprise the Sherwood Sandstone Group, which occurs in parts of Derbyshire and Staffordshire and were laid down some 230 million years ago. These consist of a very hard pebble conglomerate reaching up to 100m in depth. The ratio between sand and gravel in these deposits varies significantly and in general the proportion of gravel is less than in the drift deposits of the main river valley. The drift deposits of the Trent Valley include all the sedimentary material laid down during the last two million years. These are made up mainly of river sands and gravels along the valley floor, usually beneath

Figure 1 Location map showing River Trent and main population centres

thick layers of alluvium, and of river terraces at various points along the river sides (Fig 3). Although the solid deposits were among the first to be worked in the Trent Valley, it is the drift deposits of the river valley and terraces which have played the more prominent role in the industrial development of the region.

The deposits take the form of river terraces (see Fig 4). These represent the remains of former floodplains created during alternating cycles in which the river cut down into the valley floor and then deposited large amounts of fluvial sediment on top of it. In this way, older deposits are left higher up on the valley sides as the river deepens its course and, over a protracted period of glacial and interglacial cycles, a staircase effect of river terraces is produced which are progressively more recently formed towards the present course of the river. The main classification of the Trent Valley river terraces has traditionally been into those in the vicinity of Newark, Nottingham, Derby and Burton upon Trent, and those in the so-called 'Lincolnshire Triangle' deposited by a former easterly course of the river.

The thickness of drift deposits varies from less than 1m to a maximum of about 10m. On average they occur to a depth of 3m and 5m and are covered to a greater or lesser degree with layers of silt, clay or other fine material collectively

Figure 2 River Trent showing main gravel-bearing tributaries

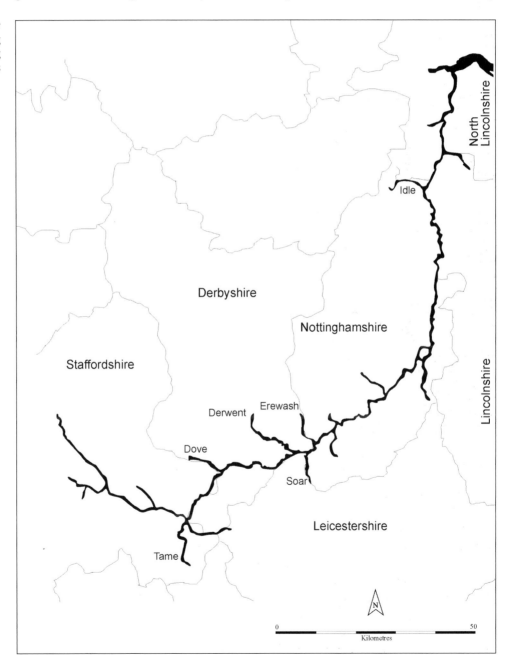

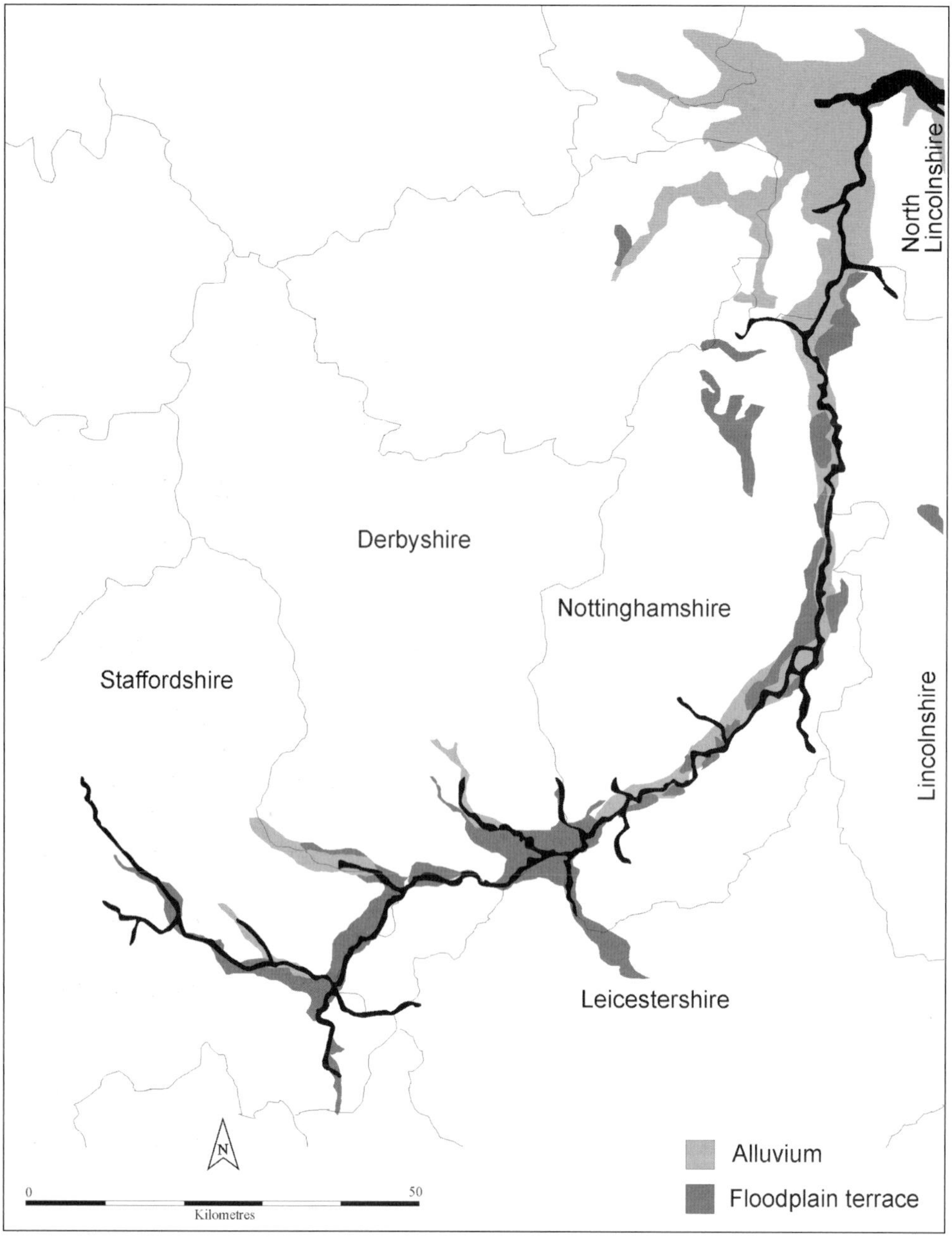

Figure 3 River Tren showing main grav deposits

Alluvium

Floodplain terrace

known as 'alluvium'. As with the solid deposits, the ratio of sand to gravel is also variable, but drift deposits typically contain smaller quantities of 'fines' (very small material). The particle size of the gravel itself is also generally smaller and more even, and it is for this reason that drift deposits are the preferred source of aggregate sand and gravel in Britain.

The first person to offer a technical definition of gravel, with characteristic attention to detail, was the pioneer geologist John Farey in his seminal *General View of the Agriculture and Minerals of Derbyshire* of 1811:

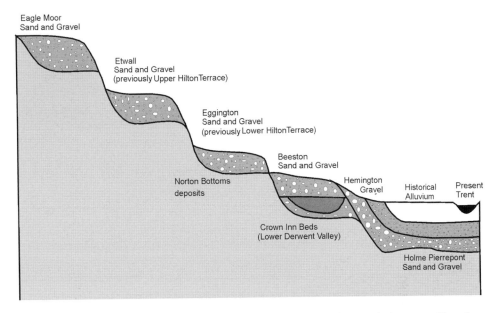

Figure 4 Schematic diagram of main Trent Valley river terraces

I use the word Gravel to express every kind of alluvia with rounded stones. If such a proportion of pebbles exist in it as is usual in gravel-pits worked for the roads, the simple term alone is sometimes used. If the stones much or very much abound, I call it clean or very clean gravel. If the earthy or loose matters in the gravel are of a sandy nature, and filter water readily, such is called either clean sandy, sandy, or very sandy gravel, according as the pebble stones are more or less abundant. If the loose matters are a mixture of sand and clay, or other earth, and filter water but imperfectly, such is either called clean loamy, loamy, or very loamy gravel. If, on the other hand, clay so abounds in gravel that water cannot filter through it, and it is difficult to separate the pebbles from the dirt, I call such either clean clayey, clayey, or very clayey gravel, according to the greater or less proportion of stones in the mass: according as quartz, flint, gritstone, limestone, toadstone, crow-stone &c. gravel.

(Farey 1811, **1**, 142)

The modern definition characterises sand and gravel deposits as accumulations of durable rock fragments and mineral grains that have been derived from the weathering and erosion of hard rocks, in particular by glacial and fluvial action, but also by that of wind. The general composition of sand and gravel deposits within a river basin reflects that of the rocks in the upland areas of the river's drainage region. So, whilst Thames Valley gravels are composed mainly of flint from the chalk uplands of the south-east of England, those of the Trent Valley contain a high proportion of quartzite pebbles derived from the Triassic Sherwood Sandstone Group of the North Midlands. For industrial purposes, sand and gravel is further defined by particle size. British concreting standard BS 882, amended since 2004 by EU regulations, defines gravel (more properly 'coarse aggregate') as particles between 4mm and 80mm in diameter. Sand (or fine aggregate) includes material smaller than 4mm but larger than 0.063mm.

By common agreement, the best deposits in the Trent Valley, to be found in a zone between Burton upon Trent and Sutton-on-Trent, about eight miles north of Newark, consist mainly of a particularly hard quartzite material ranging in size from 20mm down to 5mm. The spectacular rise of the aggregates industry in the second half of the twentieth century can be largely attributed to the particular suitability of this material to modern construction

Figure 5 Raw material of Trent Valley 'Twenty to Five' at Hoveringham Quarry (Photo: Tim Cooper/ARCUS)

techniques. Within the industry, until the recent amendment to the technical definition, it has traditionally been known by the measurements which define it: Trent Valley 'Twenty to Five' (Fig 5).

Early use of sand and gravel resources

The first clear evidence of the use of gravel resources in the Trent Valley, which is to be found in legal documents of the medieval and Elizabethan periods, suggests that they were probably used for minor land improvement schemes. Whatever the precise use, the very fact that gravel pits are mentioned in charters and deeds shows that the resource was viewed as a significant element of landed wealth. One such document, of 1589, refers to 'gravel beds' at Aston-upon-Trent, suggesting the exploitation of significant tracts of material located close to, or within, the river.

By the early 18th century the extent of gravel use was increasing, as shown by the rents paid for extraction of material from the Trent near Chilwell in 1704 and the lease of gravel beds at Weston- and Aston-upon-Trent, Wilne and Shardlow in 1709 (Fig 6). At this time the material would have been used mainly for local road improvements and was usually taken from the river, though the solid deposits in the vicinity of Normacot, to the south-east of Stoke-on-Trent, were also being exploited by this time. On the other side of the Trent, gravel quarries in the grounds of Trentham Hall were being leased in 1770 and a gravel pit had been opened up on the Mainwarings' Whitmore estate at Acton by the end of the 18th century (Fig 7). When offered for sale in 1801 it was described as 'A small piece of land, and a Gravel Pit adjoining the same, at Acton near Whitmore, in the County of Stafford, belonging to Edward Mainwaring Esq., 1801. [The pit] contains one rood and eight perches of land [and is valued] at £60 per acre'. Gradually enlarged, this pit was the longest-lived gravel working in the Trent Valley, in continuous use until 1989.

Figure 6 Principal
sites mentioned in
the text

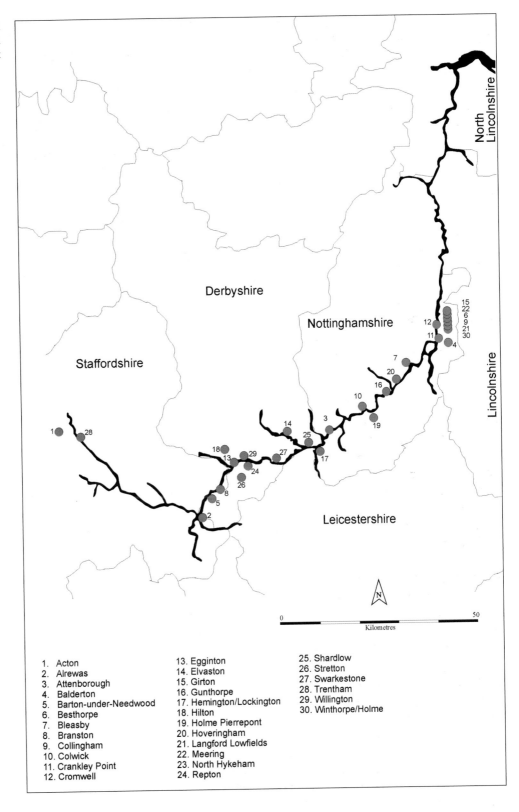

1. Acton
2. Alrewas
3. Attenborough
4. Balderton
5. Barton-under-Needwood
6. Besthorpe
7. Bleasby
8. Branston
9. Collingham
10. Colwick
11. Crankley Point
12. Cromwell
13. Egginton
14. Elvaston
15. Girton
16. Gunthorpe
17. Hemington/Lockington
18. Hilton
19. Holme Pierrepont
20. Hoveringham
21. Langford Lowfields
22. Meering
23. North Hykeham
24. Repton
25. Shardlow
26. Stretton
27. Swarkestone
28. Trentham
29. Willington
30. Winthorpe/Holme

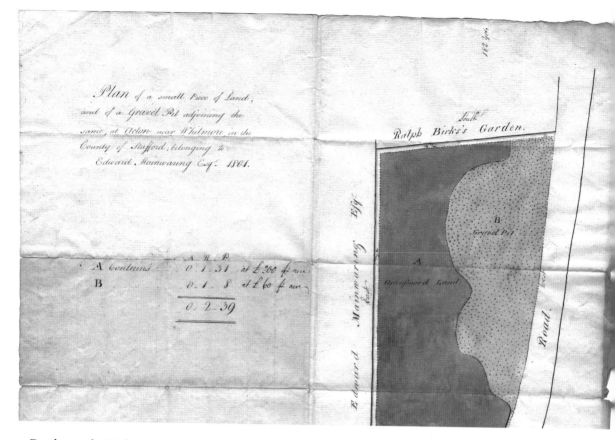

By the early 19th century the use of gravel in improving the country's ailing road system was being actively promoted. In an entry in his parish book for July 1807 the Revd Abraham Youle, rector of West Retford, drafted an article on the subject of '... observations on the forming and the repairing of roads with gravel'; this was one of a number of similar entries which show him to have been an active and practically minded social improver. Sand, gravel and clay pits were being worked at around this time in the vicinity of Alrewas, mainly for use in construction work on the Lichfield to Alrewas turnpike road and near Burton upon Trent for the Burton to Lichfield road. With his eye for detail it is not surprising that John Farey was soon calling for an application of rigorous method to the use of gravel in the roads of the Midlands and further afield:

Figure 7 Plan of Edward Mainwaring's gravel pit at Acton in 1801, worked until 1986 (Reproduced by permission of the Staffordshire Record Office)

In applying this useful material to the roads, I observe in general two principal defects. First, the gravel was rarely sufficiently clean sifted, and second the larger smooth, round stones therein were not broken, as they ought to be ... which in that state can never wedge and fix down along with the others ... In crossing Mansfield Forest from Newark, in the Autumn of 1797, I observed, about two miles from Mansfield, a considerable length of new road that had been formed, at considerable expense, entirely of smooth, round, quartz pebbles, from the size of pullets to geese eggs. Yet the difficulty, and almost impossibility, of travelling on these was so apparent that no teams had ventured on them in the course of several months, but the carters chose rather to fly off to new tracks in the deep sand and loose pebbles of the forest, for avoiding this loose pebble road, which for ages to come might remain thus unused, unless covered first by the blowing sand of the forest, or that all the largest and smoothest of the pebbles were broken with hammers into several pieces, so that their new surfaces might wedge together and fasten; in which case, no materials in Britain would make a better road ... it is surprising that this very simple method of making good gravel roads has not been more generally thought of and practised.

(Farey 1817, **3**, 250–1)

Some local landowners were already starting to see the practical, and increasingly the commercial, benefits of gravel quarrying. One who particularly caught Farey's eye was Francis Mundy Esq of Markeaton, in the Derbyshire village of Mackworth, who:

has a large gravel-pit north-west of the village where labourers are employed in the winter season in digging and sifting large stacks of gravel, levelling the rubbish, and regularly returning the top-soil on to it as the work proceeds, by which operation the land is improved greatly, and this gravel he sells to the Surveyors of the Turnpike and other Roads at 1s. per cart-load of twenty bushels. I heartily wish that this practice of Mr. Mundy ... was more generally followed by Gentlemen, who might thus do a vast deal of good, by employing the poor when short of work, and confer on the Country and themselves the benefit of good roads, often without the least loss, but some benefit to their Estates, and might even draw a small profit from the gravel, if they thought fit.

(Farey 1817, **3**, 251–2)

However, the gravel which was dredged from the Trent at places such as Laneham and Rolleston by the mid-19th century was more commonly used for the creation of paths and drives for the country houses of the gentry. At Rolleston, agents of the Manners Sutton family of Kelham Hall started issuing permits for the removal of gravel from the Trent, one boat-load at a time, a system in use up to the 1880s. Gravel was also being sold from sites in the vicinity of Farndon and South Muskham at this time, and receipts of sales from the gravel quarries at Trentham Park show that the market was gradually expanding. Between 1887 and 1892, as well as being used by the local water works company, gravel was sold to the Duke of Westminster and the Bishop of Shrewsbury, demonstrating how far high-quality material could travel. Within the next 20 years the ever-growing number of customers for Trentham Park gravel included the local police, golf clubs, telephone exchange and schools, as well as both private and public road-building schemes. An increasingly sophisticated production system saw material being screened and sold in a variety of sizes and qualities.

The increasing amount of gravel being dredged from the river up and down the valley was causing a commensurate amount of damage to its banks, a situation which led to official complaints from riverside landowners at Thrumpton and Sawley in 1838. By the end of the 19th century, however, a small number of sand

and gravel operators regularly advertising in the local directories – men such as John Thorley at Beeston, William Chapman at Newark and J A Antcliff of Sutton-on-Trent – reflect the move from the harder-won upland gravels, such as those at Acton, towards the relatively easier pickings of the river terraces.

Riches from the river bed

Ironically, the main driving force for the transition of sand and gravel extraction from local, small-scale enterprise to industrial concern was the discovery in the Trent Valley of deposits of another mineral: coal. In the years before the start of the First World War the Trent Navigation Co (henceforth 'Trent Navigation') made a series of concerted attempts to lease rights to mineral extraction from the bed of the River Trent from the Crown. The subsequent joint action by the Crown and Trent Navigation followed positive prospecting for coal in the vicinity of Torksey. Before any landowner could begin the process of extraction, the question of legal title to the river bed would need to be settled. However, the immediate effect of the letters sent by the company to local landowners, intending to make the company's case, was to stir up a hornet's nest.

In November 1908 one such landowner, Mrs Emily Cracroft-Amcotts of Kettlethorpe Hall, near Newark, wrote to the company to complain about the actions of gravel-dredging boats from Hull. These, she claimed, had dug a hole 50 feet deep in the river bed between Laughterton and Laneham Marshes which was likely to cause serious damage to the artificial river banks in the vicinity. Despite a denial from Trent Navigation that they had any connection with the dredgers, the complaint from Kettlethorpe prompted other riverside landowners, some of whom had already started attempting to charge the dredger skippers for any gravel removed, to support her cause. Their resulting joint action claimed that the Crown had no title to the river bed, which in fact belonged to individual landowners through precedent of charging for gravel removal from time immemorial. Years of dispute between the company and local landowners ensued as the company refused either to accept liability for any damage caused by dredging or to pay royalties for gravel thus removed, since in its view no royalty was payable to landowners as the bed of a tidal river was *de facto* property of the Crown. Despite the fact that the joint action between Trent Navigation and the Crown was eventually dropped, in 1921, the case had alerted commercial interests within the region that coal was not the only valuable commodity to lie beneath the waters of the Trent.

One of the first to act was the Lincoln and Hull Water Transport Company (henceforth 'Lincoln and Hull'), which built up a large fleet of steam-powered barges, or 'gravellers', between the two World Wars. One of their early employees was John 'Durgin' Thornhill, who had worked on Trent barges and gravellers since he was twelve years old, in the mid-1920s. He was born at Laneham into a family with a long association with the river:

> My grandfather had a gang of men at Laneham who used to wind the gravel in on the barge. They would pan the gravel into the barges; there were no cranes or

anything like that. They had a *trapping boat* at Laneham that had lines from it and they would get gravel with their boat and load it on to the barges from Hull.

From the early 1930s, Durgin Thornhill and his brother Frank gained some renown on the river downstream from Newark for their successful prospecting for gravel. One of the deepest deposits they found was just upriver of Cromwell Lock at a place known to the river men, owing to a prominent landmark, as 'Crow Tree'. The men measured the depth of the gravel under the river bed relative to the length of the mechanical grab mounted to their boat. In the words of Durgin's nephew Jack, 'You dig a hole and it keeps getting bigger and you start to get the marl; then you know you've got all the gravel'.

Durgin Thornhill's father and grandfather went on to pioneer the use of a custom-built gravel pan with which they would scoop material onto barges. This consisted of a leather bag or load on a metal frame mounted on a wooden shaft about 7m long. The men would push this pole into gravel deposits in the river bed and pull it up by hand. When raised, a chain released a false bottom in the bag, emptying the gravel onto the deck. Originally this work was done by hand though later, when the Thornhills were working for 'Lincoln and Hull', a steam engine and winch was employed to pull the pan out of the water. The pan would hold about eight hundredweight of material, and after it was emptied the winch would be put out of gear and the pole would be dragged back to the stern of the boat. It was then allowed to sink to the bottom and the process would start again.

Home-spun operations such as this were soon being superseded by more systematic extraction methods carried out mainly by the use of steam cranes attached to a chain and grab. Another significant technological innovation of this period was the multibucket dredger, which was mounted on the back of a barge or pontoon and excavated directly from the river bed. This process was first introduced on a large scale by Robert Teale of Carlton-on-Trent during the mid-1920s. However, when river-bed deposits became exhausted, the same method started to be employed towards the river banks, a type of operation that began to cause concern to the River Trent Catchment Board. Using multibucket dredgers, operators would eat into the bank to form a 'wet pit' connected by a narrow waterway to the main river. The ground on top ('overburden') would be removed by mechanical excavators operating from the bank, stacked to await completion of gravel working and then used to fill in the gap to the river, leaving a lagoon in the washlands. The gravel was loaded directly into barges for shipment to washing and screening plants at Hull and Grimsby. While there were few instances of serious flooding being caused by such methods, this system soon came under close scrutiny and by the mid-1940s had been prohibited for new operations on the river. According to Derrick 'Deg' Bellamy, who worked at quarries at Besthorpe and Girton:

> [Operators] were only supposed to get this gravel from the middle of the river because if you went to the sides it would let the banks in. But at night they would go to the side. The river police would come two or three times a week, up to the Humber and back

Jack Thornhill was one of the early pioneers of gravel winning through the river bank:

> There were two quarries that were allowed to go straight out of the Trent into the field; one was Winthorpe and the other was Crankley Point, just outside Newark. We changed the entrance from the river to Winthorpe pit so that it wouldn't do so much damage to the bank. There was no processing plant at Winthorpe, it was just *all ups* [raw ballast] which were sent by boat to Hull where it was processed. We never had any trouble with the river authorities. We knew them, they were reasonable people. They used to confide in us and ask if things were OK, whether we'd seen any trouble, because they wouldn't know!

The great increase in the number of sand, gravel and concrete operators during the 1920s and 1930s included some companies, such as Trent Gravels at Attenborough, Trent Concrete of Colwick, Hilton Gravel and the Midland Gravel Co, that went on to be significant players within the industry. The more successful companies were soon seeking wider markets for their material, which included pre-cast concrete products. By 1930, Trent Concrete Co was claiming that its gravel treatment plant by the riverside at Colwick was the largest in the country, and products made there included moulded concrete windowsills, fancy items such as balustrades, garden furniture, and tracery windows for

Figure 8 Trent Concrete's cast concrete works beside the Trent at Colwick, *c* 1930 (By courtesy of QMJ Publishing Ltd)

ecclesiastical use as well as the more prosaic concrete cattle stands and gateposts (Fig 8). After being dredged from the river, up to 5000 tons of material could be stored in riverside silos and up to 60 tons was being processed each hour.

However, as river-bed supplies became exhausted, and the technology required to dig land-based gravel improved, the use of the Trent itself as the main source of aggregate supply declined and, with it, the emphasis on markets on the Humber estuary. Gradually the focus of exploitation shifted from river dredging upriver of Newark to excavation of terrace deposits between Nottingham and Burton upon Trent. Trent Gravels began working a deposit situated between the river Trent and the Nottingham to Leicester railway line at Attenborough in the late 1920s. By early in 1930 this was producing close to its capacity of 75 tons per hour, and within a few years of commencing operations the plant was producing up to 7000 tons of material per week. The demand for concrete aggregate for metalled road construction promoted increasingly hectic activity in the 1930s and other companies such as Acme, with plants at Dunkirk and Nottingham, and the Hilton and Willington companies were soon joining the scramble to serve the Nottingham, Derby and Leicester markets.

The emergence of gravel production at an industrial level was reflected in the foundation of a journal, *Cement Lime and Gravel*, which from 1925 reflected the new business confidence of the aggregates operators. Five years later the Sand and Gravel Association of Great Britain (SAGA) was formed to represent the industry's interests to a wider audience and to promote co-operation between operators on matters of common interest. Within 30 years, SAGA was representing some 700 firms operating at about twice as many pits throughout England and Wales. From a national level of two million tons in 1919, production of sand and gravel increased to 20 million by 1938 and in just 20 years a small-scale activity carried out by workers on the landed estates and river boatmen had become the second most significant extractive industry in the country after coal.

The golden age of gravel

At the beginning of the 20th century sand and gravel production in the Trent Valley was little more than a by-product of estate and river management. During the course of the century it was to become, quite literally, the foundation of British economic development. The cause of this remarkable transformation in the significance of a seemingly insignificant commodity can be summed up in a single word: *concrete*.

It was the Romans who first used concrete as a durable building material on a large scale. One of the first major public works to use it in industrial quantities was the Eifel Aqueduct, constructed in AD 80 to take water some 95km from the Eifel hills in what is now Germany to the Roman city on the site of present-day Cologne. The structure was in almost continual use for a little under 200 years until its destruction during tribal warfare and subsequent robbing for reuse. When the composition of the concrete was analysed in the 1930s it was found to consist of crushed limestone with a quartz sand and hydraulic lime mortar, remarkably similar to its modern equivalent.

Indeed, it was to be another seventeen centuries before further advances were made in the use of a material still known as 'Roman cement'. In 1824 these developments led to the patenting of the first 'Portland cement' (so-called because of its similarity in colour to Portland stone) by Joseph Aspdin, a former bricklayer from Leeds who claimed to have been using the material since 1811. The first clinkered cement, in which the raw materials are fired at a higher temperature, as is the case today, was produced by Isaac Johnson at Swanscombe (Kent) in 1845. The main process which, with the addition of durable aggregate would lead to modern concrete, had been discovered.

The ready-mix revolution

The vast majority of concrete, however, was still mixed by hand on site when in 1916 Stephan Stepanian of Columbus, Ohio, filed a patent for a 'truck mixer', whereby material could be combined in transit. Although it was another ten years before a commercially viable design emerged, the concept took hold with remarkable speed and by 1929 there were well over 100 concrete mixing plants operating throughout the USA. In Britain, the person credited with providing the impetus for what became known as the 'ready-mixed concrete' industry was the Danish engineer Kjeld Ammentorp. In 1930 Ammentorp formed a company called Ready Mixed Concrete Ltd and built the country's first plant at Bedfont, near Staines (Middx). Operations there, together with the name, were taken over by an Australian company in 1952, which as the British-owned RMC Group went on to gain prominence within the industry in this country. Among the vanguard of ready-mixed concrete operators in the 1930s was Trent Gravels Ltd of Attenborough, near Nottingham; the company had begun extracting river sand and gravel in the Trent Valley in 1929 and set up its first ready-mixed concrete plant ten years later. At the outbreak of the Second World War, Trent Gravels was one of only about half a dozen operators in Britain.

The principle behind this new development in concrete production was to supply the material to uniform laboratory specifications in the required quantity in a condition for immediate use. The revolutionary nature of the development, apart from the convenience of delivery, is that it ensured uniformity of mix, and therefore consistency of strength, as well as providing a workable mixture for the duration of a job. As such, the development of ready-mixed concrete provided the impetus for the large-scale construction and road-building programmes which characterised global economic development in the second half of the twentieth century. Locally, the coincidence of the development of ready-mixed concrete technology with the outbreak of war provided a significant boost to the aggregates industry in the Trent Valley, well-placed as it was to contribute to defence works in the midlands and east of England. Additionally, a technology dependent on uniform durable aggregate provided a ready market for the hard quartzite gravels of the Trent Valley.

The defence impetus

In common with 20th-century developments in heavy industry generally, it was war and the preparations for it which provided the stimulus for the nascent concrete industry and that of sand and gravel production on which it depended. By the late 1930s runways, bunkers, air-raid shelters, gun emplacements, and parking areas for military vehicles were all consuming huge quantities of Trent Valley aggregates. In particular, the airfield construction programme led to a rapid expansion of the industry from 1938 onwards, especially marked in the so-called 'Lincolnshire Triangle'. Construction peaked in the first half of 1943, when large numbers of former grass airfields were converted to concrete for the accommodation of heavy bombers and bases in Yorkshire and Lincolnshire were taking delivery of massive quantities of aggregate each day. Further afield, Hoveringham Gravel Co (later Hoveringham Gravels Ltd) was delivering all through the night the vast quantities of material required for new extended concrete runways at Alconbury airfield in Cambridgeshire (Fig 9). These became necessary following the transference of the base to the USAAF, which was commencing missions with the huge B-24 'Liberator' and B-17 'Flying Fortress' bombers.

Another significant consequence of the wartime demand was the general shift from the small-scale river-dredging operations characteristic of the early industry to full exploitation of the high-quality, easily attainable terrace gravels. Output from river dredging, which reached a peak of 218,000 cubic yards per annum in 1943, fell to just 60,000 in 1946. Conversely, between 1938 and 1943, output from the Nottingham terraces rose from 376,000 cubic yards to 621,000 and from the Derby and Burton terraces from 278,000 to 425,000.

In the Trent Valley the main players at the outbreak of war were all members of the Midland Gravels Association: Branston Gravels, Burton and Branston Sand and Gravel Co, Derbyshire Gravel and Aggregates (Repton), Hilton Gravel, Trent Gravels (Attenborough) and Willington Gravels at Egginton. Quarries at Winthorpe, Besthorpe, Crankley Point and Hoveringham all commenced operations in or around September 1939 to meet demand for the airfields, factories and roads which contributed to the war effort. In addition, smaller pits

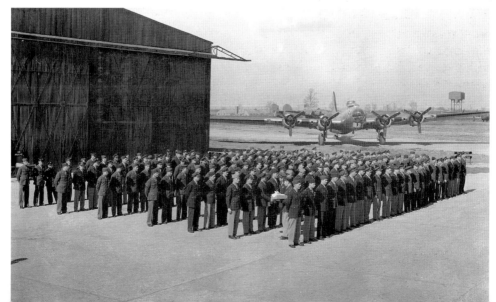

Figure 9 Concrete runway built with Hoveringham gravel, USAAF Alconbury, 1943. The heavy-duty runways were required for aircraft such as the B17 'Flying Fortress' (in background of the photograph)

took part in the manufacture of sandbags for the protection of buildings in Hull, Grimsby and other urban centres within reach of barge traffic from the Trent.

In the early months of the war, gravel quarry workers were among those called up for service, but, like coal mining, the aggregates industry soon came under reserved occupation regulations. An early indication of this development was the virtual assumption of control of ready-mixed concrete operations at Trent Gravels' works at Attenborough by the nearby Chilwell Ordnance Depot. The close association between the war effort and the emerging gravel industry was further exemplified, albeit on a smaller scale, by the use of the worked-out pit at Hilton as a rifle range by the Home Guard. The peak of the industry's development during this period coincided with the conclusion of the main airfield construction programme in 1943, and, following a small rise in demand leading up to the D-Day operations of the following year, output fell rapidly: in the Trent Valley as a whole from a level of 3.6 million cubic yards in 1943 to 1.6 million in 1946.

The squire's tale: Hilton Gravels Ltd

The Hilton Gravel company was established by local landowner James Marston Spurrier of Marston Hall, Hilton, in 1924. Extraction on the Hilton site had commenced under his father in the late 19th century with a workforce of half a dozen men using shovels. The material was then screened using a simple hand riddle and was sold mainly for footpaths and drives for larger houses. This was a market which Mr Spurrier continued to exploit in the 1920s, at the same time as expanding production to include crushed and washed gravel for use in concrete. By this time material was being excavated by steam shovel and taken to the processing plant by horse-drawn railway wagons. This was later replaced by a diesel loco system.

As was typical of sand and gravel firms formed during this period, the company was boosted by a surge in demand during the Second World War, and in 1948 produced 80,000 cubic yards of sand and gravel from the original quarry alone. The main working face at this time comprised a seam about 5m in depth, covering an area of around 89 acres. An additional deposit was then being worked by dragline excavator at Hemington Fields near Shardlow, producing a further 105,000 cubic yards a year. An even larger unit, covering an area of 113 acres at Stretton, near Burton upon Trent, was producing 96,000 cubic yards per annum. The company also had a quarry at Willington, from which material was conveyed by road to the main plant at Hilton for processing (Fig 10). The firm had already branched out into pre-cast concrete products, mainly for the local agricultural market, and tennis court surfacings, although its core business remained the traditional one of material for drives and paths. The local importance of the 'Hilcrete' concrete subsidiary is attested to by the number of surviving concrete gate-posts in the locality bearing the monogram 'JMS' after the company's founder (Fig 11).

Figure 10 Hilton Gravel's Hemington works in the 1950s (Reproduced by permission of the Record Office for Leicestershire, Leicester and Rutland)

Figure 11 Concrete gatepost with 'JMS' monogram, Ivy House Farm, Marston on Dove (Photo: Andrew Cliff)

By the end of the 1950s the company had assembled a fleet of 200 lorries and, with additional quarries at Willington, Mercaston and Kirk Ireton in Derbyshire, and Longton near Stoke-on-Trent, was one of the largest quarry owners and suppliers of sand and gravel in the North and East Midlands. At this time it had commenced ready-mixed concrete operations at a number of plants in the Greater Manchester area. In the mid-1960s production started of specialist material, mainly from the Hemington quarry, delivered for horticultural and golf-course use throughout the UK as well as abroad. The company's success led, in 1967, to acquisition by the Blue Circle Aggregates Group, whose parent company was taken over by the French company, Lafarge, in 2001.

'Planning for peace'

The sand and gravel industry's expansion in the five years between 1938 and 1943 had been extremely rapid, yet the slump in the second half of the 1940s was almost equal in its severity. Despite the urgent need for the reconstruction of bombed cities – locally this applied in particular to the Nottingham and Humber conurbations – national infrastructure was too weak to provide the industry with the high levels of demand of the war years. However, the post-war government, highly attuned to ideas of public planning that had served the country so well in time of war, was certain that steps needed to be taken to secure the future of what was now seen as a prime national industry.

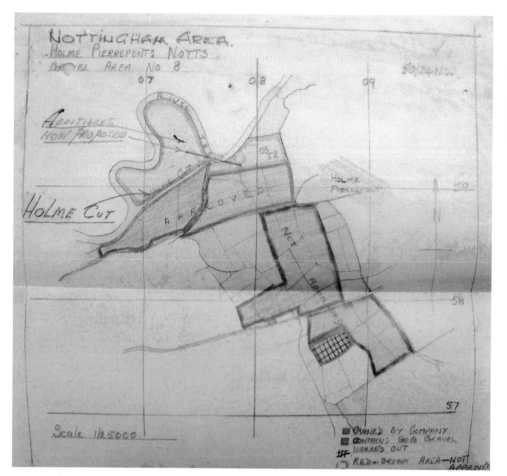

Figure 12 Plan of Holme Pierrepont Quarry drawn up for the Waters Committee (Reproduced by permission of The National Archives; MAF 141/155)

The Waters Report

Investigation into the mineral sector by the Ministry of Town and Country Planning began in 1943 and consisted of ministerial discussions with representatives of the Ballast, Sand and Allied Trades Association (BSATA). A particular encouragement to the industry was the government's sympathy to the perceived need to bypass local planning blockages which, it was argued, were detrimental to its recovery and sustained development. Against a backdrop of fears among the agriculture lobby of the effects of unregulated gravel production, the Advisory Committee on Sand and Gravel was set up in June 1944 under the chairmanship of Major A H S Waters.

The main responsibilities of what became known as the Waters Committee were to consider the maintenance of adequate supplies at a reasonable cost, the avoidance of unnecessary disturbance to high-quality agricultural land, and the co-ordination of sand and gravel working with other land uses. For the government's part, one of the main tasks was to attempt to predict, as accurately as possible, the trajectory of demand for aggregates over the next half-century. Organisations consulted by the committee included the Council for British Archaeology, the

Council for the Preservation of Rural England, the County Councils Association, the River Boards Association and the National Farmers' Union. Already, by the end of the Second World War, the Trent Valley was taking its place as one of the most important areas of sand and gravel production in the country. It was a reflection of the industry's extraordinary growth that the area was selected for special review by the Committee. In the words of the chairman:

> Our reasons were two: that the stretch of the Trent Valley now under review has a larger gross output than any other comparable tract, and for that reason ranks second only to the London area in the general view of the industry and, secondly, that the quality of the Trent Valley [gravels] is so high, and their location relative to the great industrial markets of the Midlands so crucial, that it seemed to us desirable to emphasise the importance of continued production in this vital area.
>
> (Waters Report Part 3, pp 10–11)

At an early stage in its deliberations the committee felt that existing production and market zones in the Trent Valley were sufficiently developed that they should not be interfered with. Instead, the region was divided into 'service areas' based on centres at Burton upon Trent, Newark, Nottingham and Lincoln. The committee set to work towards producing estimates of future demand and allocations of reserves in each of these areas and highlighted the need for the production of a detailed map of sand and gravel resources. The committee was also of the opinion that planning policy should work towards large plants rather than allowing a proliferation of smaller workings which was likely to be detrimental on grounds of both economy and land use. However, local planning authorities (LPAs) were to be given flexibility in granting permissions for working in order to discourage the formation of monopolies, an important principle which the report referred to as 'elbow room' (Waters Report Part 3, p 75).

During the course of 1948, sand and gravel operators throughout the country were sent questionnaires asking for details of their production and reserves. It was at this stage that the committee first called for discussion by interested parties of the possibility of a levy on sand and gravel production to raise funds for the restoration of worked-out sites. However, in the light of significant disagreement between representatives of industry and local government, the proposals were subsequently dropped.

The committee's report was published in eighteen parts between 1948 and 1955. These dealt with each gravel region in turn, indicating those areas where some future working might take place and those which should be reserved for agriculture (Fig 12). In addition, the report made an estimation of demand for sand and gravel up to the end of the twentieth century. A significant general conclusion concerned the different approach that was to be taken to the country's two main gravel regions. In particular, the committee based its recommendations for the London area on the possibility that large parts of the gravel field would be exhausted well before the expiry of the 50-year forecast period. In the Trent Valley, by contrast, the main challenge was considered to be the allocation of sufficient gravel-producing land to allow existing production centres to at least maintain their rate of output and, in some cases, to significantly expand. The report concluded with a brief consideration of the situation that was expected to follow the 50-year forecast period:

> ... although there is no reason to suppose that demand for gravel will decline, and since substantial tracts of the gravel field will still remain unworked ... precise recommendations as to the location of future workings would be unduly speculative ... We have preferred therefore not to try to forecast the shape of the industry in the twenty-first century, confident that changes of focus during the next few decades will by then have brought the picture into sharper definition.
>
> (Waters Report, Part 3, p 11)

The Town and Country Planning Act

Following intense lobbying by the industry, government soon set about addressing perceived 'log jams' in the planning process by sending out directives to local authorities. In a move designed to placate hostile reactions on the part of local authorities, developing policy included moves to introduce rating of surface mineral workings. The Waters Report's recommendation that Local Development Plans should be produced by planning authorities was implemented, with the further recommendation that an industry levy should be paid direct to the new Local Planning Authorities to allow them to take responsibility for the restoration of old workings; this was, however, a suggestion which was rejected by LPA representatives. In 1947 the Town and Country Planning Act established procedure for the granting of planning permission for all forms of development, including the opening and working of sand and gravel pits, and continued to provide the basis of minerals legislation up to the end of the century.

Mapping the resource

In the aftermath of the upsurge in demand for gravel during in the early 1940s, the Waters Committee identified resource location as one of the most important challenges facing the industry and planners. The geological maps available at that time showing 'drift' deposits were not available for the whole country; indeed, they were missing for entire aggregates-rich areas such as the Cheshire Plain and the West Riding of Yorkshire. In fact, it was not until the early 1960s, when government planning and the construction boom were in full swing, that it was decided to initiate economic surveys of mineral resources with the aim of obtaining the fullest possible information on deposits of sand and gravel not already in the control of the industry. Under the direction of the Ministry of Housing and Local Government, the first map of sand and gravel distribution was published in the autumn of 1965 in the 1:635,000 National Planning series of maps of Great Britain under the auspices of the Ordnance Survey.

In addition to the maps now available to potential and existing operators, section 103 of the Town and Country Planning Act (1947) empowered the relevant government authorities and LPAs to authorise entry on to any land for prospecting and boring for minerals, although in practice such rights were only granted in connection with formal applications for planning permission. Between the 1960s and early 1990s a series of detailed sand and gravel resource maps were published. This was followed, between the mid-1990s and 2006, by a series of county-wide mineral resource maps produced by the British Geological Survey for the purpose of guiding planning departments.

Conflict with agriculture

Acclaim for the rapid development of the Trent Valley sand and gravel industry during the 1930s had not been universal. The local agricultural community – which included mixed and dairy farmers in the Burton to Newark zone, cattle farmers north of Newark and both arable and sheep farmers to the east of the Trent – had been viewing developments with increasing concern. In 1939 this had led to a full-scale investigation by the Ministry of Agriculture which concluded:

> that from the agricultural point of view [the Ministry] is anxious that the exploitation of the terrace gravels should be limited as far as possible and that gravel working should be diverted to the plateau and glacial gravels. This conclusion applies with particular force to the terrace gravels.
>
> (National Archives WORK 45/205)

However, this statement did little to ease the tensions that were often apparent between local farmers and quarry owners and, increasingly, between the 'rival' ministries of Agriculture and Housing within government itself. In the wake of the 1946 review of gravel production in the Thames Valley, which recommended that much highly fertile market-garden land be preserved, Nottinghamshire farmers lobbied government concerning their own fears over loss of high-quality terrace pasture to gravel working. The response, in the form of the Waters recommendations, was not entirely welcome. Whereas for the Thames Valley certain parts of the gravel field were to be reserved for agriculture, no such guarantee was to be forthcoming for the Trent region. In its review of the local gravel industry the committee made its position regarding the conflicting requirements of agriculture and aggregates quite clear:

> There is a fundamental distinction between this region [the Trent Valley] and the lower Thames. Although the area of the workable gravel field here is much larger, we do not think that a realistic solution of the problem can be found without admitting from the beginning that some of the meadow land will have to be worked for gravel if supplies are to be maintained at a reasonable price.
>
> (Waters Report Part 3, p 23)

Set in concrete: Trent Gravels Ltd

The Attenborough quarry of Trent Gravels Ltd was opened in 1929 on a site between the River Trent and the Nottingham–Leicester railway line. The company founders were a consortium of six Nottinghamshire businessmen who were encouraged by the proximity of a good gravel deposit to potentially lucrative markets in the Derby/Nottingham industrial conurbation. For distribution purposes the plant was deliberately sited as close to the railway line as possible. Extraction was originally by means of suction-dredger, which was capable of producing an average of 75 tons of material per hour. In the busy summer season the plant was soon working double shifts, resulting in a weekly output of 7000 tons of sand and gravel. In 1939 the pump system was replaced by dragline excavators loading onto barges which conveyed the material to the processing plant through the worked-out lagoons. In the same year the company commenced ready-mixed concrete operations, initially as a means of shoring up the sand and gravel business and, potentially, extending it. At this time, there were only about three other suppliers of ready-mixed concrete in the UK, and in the East Midlands region Trent Gravels enjoyed a complete monopoly until 1958.

The outbreak of the Second World War brought new impetus to the company in the form of demand for concrete bunkers, shelters, runways and holding areas for military equipment. Being sited within a mile of the Ministry of Defence's Chilwell Ordnance Depot, the Attenborough works soon came under the effective control of the local commanding officer of the Royal Engineers and its small workforce was immediately placed on the list of reserved occupations. At the end of the war, Trent Gravels was still one of only four firms supplying truck-mixed concrete in the whole of the country (Fig 13). This part of the business expanded rapidly in the 1950s with demand for concrete for new council housing, road and bridge improvements in the Nottingham area. Further afield, the disastrous floods of 1953 meant that Trent Gravels concrete mixers were taking material all the way to the east coast for emergency sea defences.

In 1961 the company went into partnership with another local firm, Trent Concrete Ltd of Colwick, to form a distribution company, Trent Ready Mixed Concrete Ltd, under the joint ownership of both companies. Competition between the two was kept to a minimum by apportioning the trade on a geographical basis. The 1960s and early 1970s were a boom time for construction work, which included, locally, the M1 motorway, new buildings for the University of Nottingham and University Hospital, and the development of many private housing estates and inner-city multistorey rehousing schemes. A notable contract undertaken by the company was Nottingham's new Playhouse Theatre, which won architectural awards for its use of exposed concrete for both external and internal decoration (Fig 14).

In the mid-1960s sand and gravel production was based on two plants at the Attenborough site with a combined output of 200 tons per hour, and a concrete plant capable of producing 60 cubic yards per hour. The company had its own fleet of vehicles and production of sand and gravel rose from just under 220,000 tons in 1958 to almost 490,000 in 1967. By this time almost all production was going into the manufacture of concrete, the earlier market for gravel road surfacings having shrunk considerably in the face of developing asphalt technology. Following criticism of the impact of its gravel workings on the local environment, the company became increasingly involved in the creation of what is now Attenborough Nature Reserve. Opened in 1966 by the celebrated naturalist David Attenborough, this was established in an area of worked-out gravel lagoons covering an area of some 100 hectares.

Figure 13 Truck mixer leaving Trent Gravels' Attenborough plant, 1950s (By courtesy of Michael Arthur)

Figure 14 The Playhouse Theatre, Nottingham, c 1965: much-vaunted icon of decorative concrete modernism (By courtesy of Cemex UK)

At the height of its success in the late 1960s the company attracted the interest of its main rival, Hoveringham Gravels Ltd, which was then undertaking acquisition of smaller operators throughout the country. However, following the announcement by the managing director, J Stanleigh Turner, that he would never sell his company to his Hoveringham counterpart, Harold Needler, take-over speculation appeared to be quashed. There was general surprise, therefore, when the company was in fact taken over by the RMC Group in 1969. RMC was taken over in turn by the Mexican company Cemex in 2004. Subject to ongoing planning reviews, the gravel working based at Attenborough and Long Eaton has permission to continue extraction until 2024. This would mean that the site will have been in operation for almost 100 years, an impressive statistic in the context of the average life of a sand and gravel quarry of little more than ten to fifteen years.

Hard on the heels of this recommendation, however, the government issued proposals aimed at satisfying both sides. Gravel exploitation was to be concentrated first of all on the lowest-quality agricultural land in the vicinity of Newark, Lincoln and Torksey. The next zone to be worked would be the urbanised areas around Lincoln, Newark, Nottingham, Derby and Burton, especially land liable to flooding and therefore unsuitable for development. Any underlying gravel in these areas should be exploited as fully as possible, especially since the land could 'relatively easily be restored using urban refuse'. The land which should be kept from gravel exploitation the longest was to include the higher-quality arable and pasture to the north of Nottingham.

By the beginning of the 1960s the urban development boom was in full swing and any remaining dissent within the agricultural lobby went largely unheard. For its part, SAGA was keen to demonstrate its ability to work hand in hand with farming interests, a position set out in its 'Gravel Working with Agriculture' pamphlet of 1960. In spite of increasing concerns regarding the expansion of exploratory drilling activities on agricultural land, this set out the industry opinion that new planning regulations could work effectively to minimise long-term damage to agricultural interests. In the end, the hard facts of economics were most persuasive in winning the arguments, and few landowners and farmers could disregard the attraction of potentially lucrative gravel royalties. With East Midlands landowners such as the duke of Newcastle taking the lead (he was being paid royalties of around one shilling per ton as owner of the site of Girton quarry), the way was now clear for the full-scale development of the high-quality terrace gravels of the middle Trent Valley.

'Building a better Britain'

> Sand and gravel are basic to all major building and construction work. They enter into the composition of buildings of every kind, from a bungalow to an airport, and every form of road communication system from a footpath to an arterial road and an airport runway.
>
> (H E Pierce, chairman of SAGA quoted in
> *Cement Lime and Gravel*, August 1958, p 31)

In 1937, at the beginning of the modern industrial aggregates era, annual national production of gravel stood at 16 million cubic yards. In 1964 it was 90 million. These figures alone give some impression of the extent to which the modern aggregates industry emerged as a response to the construction and road-building boom of the 1950s and 60s.

By the late 1950s a small number of operators had consolidated their position in the Trent Valley region. In the Burton and Derby service areas these included Branston Gravels, Hilton Gravels (with three active pits at Hilton, Willington and Stretton), Derbyshire Gravel and Aggregates (Swarkestone), and the Drakelow Gravel Company, operating on land leased from the Central Electricity Generating Board next to the power station of the same name. In the increasingly important Nottingham Terrace area, Hilton Gravels operated a further two pits at Hemington, but the market was coming to be dominated by Trent Gravels working upriver from Attenborough towards Long Eaton, and Hoveringham Gravels, with its quarries at Bleasby, Colwick, Holme Pierrepont, and Hoveringham itself. Providing significant competition in this area was Gunthorpe Gravels. In the Newark service area the Newark Gravel Co was reaching the high point of its position in the market due to the proximity of its reserves to the built-up area of Newark. Inns and Co, based in the south-east of England, still produced significant output from its pit at Besthorpe, but again this area was increasingly dominated by Hoveringham Gravels, with its quarry at Crankley Point.

Production figures released by the government in 1960 showed that output of sand and gravel was already far exceeding the 50-year estimates that had been a prime function of the Waters Committee. In high-production areas such as the Trent Valley they were as much as three times higher. In addition to the commencement of work on the M1 motorway, ministers cited the rising amount of construction work and the development of concreting techniques as reasons for the need to revise the figures substantially upwards. By the end of 1961, total aggregate production from the Trent Valley region stood at just under 5 million cubic yards, of which the Burton and Derby Terraces accounted for about 20% and the Nottingham Terraces just over one-third. Throughout the rest of the 1960s, production levels continued to soar. The main impetus behind the explosion in demand for gravel at this time was provided by the public works, defence and reconstruction programmes initiated by government in the two decades following the end of the Second World War.

Power

An immediate consequence of post-war redevelopment was that demand for electricity doubled in the period between 1940 and 1950. Government policy was soon formulated towards replacing outdated municipal electricity generators with large-capacity power stations linked to a National Grid. The Trent Valley, commanding a ready water supply, proximity to the Nottinghamshire and Derbyshire coalfields and good rail communications, was an ideal location on which to focus the construction programme. The immediate post-war phase saw the construction of power stations at Staythorpe, High Marnham, Drakelow, Willington and Castle Donington (Fig 15). Apart from the vast amounts of concrete consumed in the construction of both power plant and cooling towers – the average cooling tower was said to require about 35,000 cubic yards of concrete – thousands of tons of sand were required simply to stabilise much of the waterlogged ground around the stations to accommodate rail facilities.

A second phase of construction up to the late 1960s saw additional units at Drakelow, Willington and Castle Donington join the grid, in addition to new plants at Rugeley and Ratcliffe-on-Soar. Gravel quarry workers in the Nottingham

area in particular testify to the impact of this intense activity on their working lives. Dorothy Winn (neé Scrivener) was an office worker at Hoveringham in the early 1950s:

Figure 15 Staythorpe Power Station, completed in 1950 (By courtesy of Balfour Beatty plc)

> Even in the office I was working from 7.30 to 5.00 and 7.30 to 1.00 on a Saturday and then I would take all the paperwork home at the end of the month, and of an evening if I was behind. We were very busy then – they built Staythorpe power-station while I was there. You had big contracts that had to be fulfilled.

A significant element of the power-station construction programme was a desire on the part of the government to co-ordinate gravel extraction, concrete production and the use of waste in the form of pulverised fuel ash (PFA) for infilling worked-out pits (see Chapter 3). The policy was not always entirely successful and often involved the use of extensive pipelines to make delivery more efficient and less of a public nuisance. Such pipelines became quite prominent features of villages such as Willington. The demise of the coal industry from the mid-1980s onwards led to the gradual decommissioning of a number of Trent Valley power stations and the conversion of others to gas. In 1998, however, the construction of a new gas-fired unit at Staythorpe was begun; this included the use of over 72,000 tonnes of sand and gravel from borrow pits in the vicinity.

Roads and runways

The post-war government's decision to develop an independent nuclear strike force came to fruition with the commissioning of the V-bomber fleet in the mid-1950s. The subsequent requirement for extended heavy-duty concrete runways was another boost to the local aggregates industry. At its peak it is estimated that airfield schemes in Lincolnshire and Yorkshire were taking deliveries of concrete at the rate of 500 tons per day, the majority of which came from pits in the Trent Valley region. The hard quartzite gravels of the Nottingham Terraces were particularly suited for runway construction. When tests were undertaken in search of an extremely durable concrete aggregate for the runways required at Filton, near Bristol, for the 'Brabazon' super-airliner, no suitable local material was found (Fig 16). Despite needing to be transported over 200km, therefore, it was material from Hoveringham that was selected for this lucrative contract. Trainloads of material were transported from a specially built unit at Thurgarton railway yard next to the quarry.

However, by the end of the 1950s, there was general recognition that further demand for airfield construction would be limited and it was on road-building schemes that the aggregates industry would come to depend. Of particular importance to the Trent Valley were the modernisation of the A1 arterial route from London to Newcastle and the East Midlands and Yorkshire sections of the M1 motorway (Fig 17). These had a huge impact on demand for local aggregates, with every mile of the A1 Newark bypass alone estimated to require 30,000 cubic yards of concrete in its construction.

The significance of the road-building programme to the fortunes of the Trent Valley aggregates industry was emphasised at the completion of the Leicestershire section of the M1 in 1966. Almost the entire aggregate requirements for this

Figure 16 The ill-fated Bristol Brabazon on the concrete runway built at Filton with Hoveringham gravel, 1949 (By courtesy of the Rolls Royce Heritage Trust)

section had been supplied from pits on the Nottinghamshire Terraces and when the motorway reached Derbyshire the replacement of gravel with local crushed limestone led to a local slump in the sand and gravel industry. High-quality Nottinghamshire gravel continued to be in demand, however, and received a welcome boost with the construction of the Humber Bridge in the late 1970s. According to Jack Thornhill:

> The best gravel was at Girton Lane End; in fact, the first two fields there were probably the best gravel along the whole length of the river. This is where the Humber Bridge gravel was taken from. What made this gravel good quality was that the stone was really hard. A lot of gravel has a lot of sand in it but gravel for big public works like aerodromes or power stations, taking 4–5 feet thick of concrete or more, needs good three-quarter inch stone. The inch-and-a-half was used for really big jobs like abutments on bridges which needed to be really hard.

Construction

Speaking at the annual dinner of the Reinforced Concrete Association in 1957, the then Minister of Works told his audience that he 'would like to see reinforced and pre-stressed concrete used to a far greater extent in the British building industry because [we are] anxious to economise in steel and to keep the cost of building as low as possible' (*The Quarry Managers' Journal*, July 1957, p 19). Following comments regarding the huge economies that could be made by

Figure 17 Trent Gravels truck mixer delivering to an M1 construction site, *c* 1965 (By courtesy of Michael Arthur)

increased use of such materials, the minister went on to suggest that this was also desirable on aesthetic grounds and argued against perceptions that concrete was an inherently drab material. Indeed, imaginative use of exposed aggregate could make buildings quite attractive. He concluded with the words 'I hope and believe that your association will continue in its good work and simultaneously provide good buildings at reasonable cost and add to the charm and beauty of our times.'

As well as setting the tone for the modernist ethos of the period, the minister's words were music to the ears of the aggregates industry which welcomed the imminent 'building revolution' with open arms. Post-war developments in concrete technology stimulated growing demand for reinforced concrete frames for large office blocks, hotels and flats as well as pre-stressed bridges and beams for aircraft hangars and factories. The atmosphere of feverish activity is recalled by Mike Arthur, who was in charge of monitoring concrete quality for Trent Gravels at Attenborough:

> In the years after the war, development in the Nottingham area was rapid: the M1 was being built, there was a new bridge over the Trent, Nottingham University was being expanded, new housing estates were going up. There was a tremendous demand for concrete so the main emphasis was on fulfilling the needs of the market while making a profit at the same time. (Fig 18)

This was a boom time exploited fully by the emerging big producers in the Nottingham region, the Hoveringham and Trent Gravels companies. Hoveringham consolidated its national position by floating on the stock exchange in 1963 at

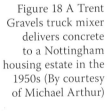

Figure 18 A Trent Gravels truck mixer delivers concrete to a Nottingham housing estate in the 1950s (By courtesy of Michael Arthur)

a time when it was operating no fewer than 30 quarries nationally and was one of the main producers for large public works contracts. By the mid-1960s, in addition to quarries in other parts of the country, the company owned eight of the 20 working pits in the Trent Valley. With an annual output approaching one million tonnes it was producing almost 10% of the country's sand and gravel, while its share of the national ready-mixed concrete market was around 25%. Trent Gravels' production of sand and gravel at the Attenborough works more than doubled between 1958 and 1967. One of the company's contracts, the new Clifton Bridge across the Trent, contained about 50,000 cubic yards of concrete alone.

The boom lasted until the late 1960s, and the aggregates industry increasingly recognised its dependence on the buoyancy of construction activity. No sooner had it done so, however, than the inevitable downturn began. In 1973 reduced demand from the construction industry initiated the first major slump in aggregates production since the end of the Second World War. For the first time since the 1930s, signs of decline in business optimism were detectable within the industry. The end of the Golden Age was in sight.

Developments in planning

One of the first consequences of the serious underestimation of demand for sand and gravel by the Waters Committee was the inauguration of a series of Trent Valley Gravel Reviews between 1956 and the mid-1960s. At this time so-called 'sand and gravel working parties' were starting to be set up for the purpose of revising government estimates of demand at local level. These provided the stimulus for the development of 'structure' and 'local' plans which became the main vehicle for delivering minerals policies up until the early 21st century. The key elements of Minerals Local Plans included making provision for adequate supply of minerals; identifying areas of possible future working; monitoring a system of reserves of land held by minerals companies with outline planning permission (so-called 'landbanks'); and balancing the need for minerals with the protection of local environment and amenities.

The most important development so far as aggregate minerals were concerned was the establishment of Regional Aggregate Working Parties (RAWPs) covering the main planning regions of England, the first to become active being that for the East Midlands, in 1974. Their role was to collect information on supply and reserves of aggregates to enable regular forecasts of requirements to be made, and to ensure that national demand was apportioned between regions. The establishment of the RAWPs coincided with the publication of the Report of the Advisory Committee on Aggregates (Verney Report) between 1976 and 1978. The committee had been established to consider the problem of maintaining supplies while minimising negative environmental and social impact. Of particular importance were its recommendations regarding the development of marine aggregate resources, the increased use of recycled material, the development of nature reserves at disused quarries and the safeguarding of archaeological resources. All of these were to have significant impact on the future shape of the industry in the Trent Valley and beyond. The coterminous Report of the Committee on Planning Control over Mineral Working (Stevens Report) recommended greater central control of minerals planning. This was rejected by government, a decision which enhanced the importance of regional and local bodies and set the tone for minerals planning for the next 30 years.

From family business to big business

Between the end of the Second World War and the late 1960s the aggregates industry developed from a predominantly family business model to one dominated by large public companies. The main impetus for this change was the need to secure large-scale capital investment both for land acquisition and to finance increasingly complex plant. The take-over trend was in full swing by the mid-1960s, at a time when the Hilton, Midland, Branston, Drakelow and Trentham gravel companies were all owned by Blue Circle Aggregates, itself part of the Associated Portland Manufacturers Group. The long-standing operator at Acton, Naybro Stone, was taken over by William Cooper & Sons in 1966, who, shortly afterwards, were taken over themselves by the RMC group. Inns and Co, which had been significant in the opening-up of quarries at Besthorpe and Collingham, was one of seventeen companies subsumed by the Redland Holdings group. The locally based Hoveringham Gravels had no fewer than 26 subsidiary companies by the late 1960s, including its former competitor the Newark Gravel and Concrete Co. In many cases takeovers were accompanied by redundancies. In some, they truly brought about the end of an era, such as at Hilton Gravel which, until its acquisition by Blue Circle, had been owned by the local squire.

A growing trend was for so-called 'vertical integration', by which companies whose main interest was in the finished product, ready-mixed concrete, bought up small aggregates companies in order to ensure ongoing supplies of raw material. At the same time there was a strong element of 'horizontal integration', whereby companies which had previously specialised in the production of, for example, crushed rock, moved into sand and gravel, and vice versa. By the late 1970s the nine largest ready-mixed concrete firms in the country together held at least 40% of its sand and gravel reserves and permission to quarry in six of the eight planning regions of England. These firms included some that would go on to dominate production in the Trent Valley to the end of the 20th century: RMC, Tarmac, ARC and Redland. Of the independent operators in the Trent Valley, only Hoveringham remained at the top table.

The backdrop to much of this take-over activity was speculation, rife since the inception of the Waters Committee, that the industry would share the fate of coal and iron and be nationalised. Each new gravel review heightened tensions among company executives who feared that the rising costs of site reclamations would play into the government's hands. Part of the remit of the 1976 Verney Report was a consideration of increased regulation of the industry in the light of depletion of reserves and growing environmental concern. In 1978 Hoveringham Gravels pledged its support to the growing anti-nationalisation campaign which went on to win the day with the Conservative general election victory of the following year.

The process of acquisition in the aggregates sector, as well as the merging of aggregates and concrete interests, continued into the 21st century, by which time the sand and gravel industry in the Trent Valley was dominated by four major concerns. Tarmac, the largest UK producer of aggregates, which had swallowed up Hoveringham in 1981, was taken over itself by the Anglo-American group in 1999. This South-African-based organisation had already subsumed the Tilcon ready-mixed concrete company and in 2007 announced its intention of offering Tarmac for sale. Hanson plc, the world's largest aggregates producer and the second biggest in the UK, took over ARC in 1990 and was itself acquired by German company HeidelbergCement (sic) in 2007. The French company Lafarge took over Redland in 1997 and RMC, the fourth-largest aggregates company in the world, was taken over in 2005 by the Mexican concern Cemex. By the summer of 2007 all the major players in the British aggregates sector were in foreign ownership and an industry with deep roots in the Trent Valley was now truly global.

A mammoth organisation: Hoveringham Gravels Ltd

Fog-bound while motoring from one of his quarries in Wakefield, Mr Harold Arnold came across a little garage and found the proprietor busily screening some dredgings from the Trent. The garage man told Mr Arnold that he knew where there was 'a million tons of gravel' if there were the facilities to exploit it. Mr Arnold had the facilities – and that is how Hoveringham started.

In a celebratory article in the *Newark Advertiser* in 1954, quarry manager Noel North recounted the origins of what was to become the largest aggregates producer in the country. Arnold, a Yorkshire civil engineer and quarry owner, had made the journey in 1938 and the gravel-bearing land in question was sandwiched between the river Trent and the main Nottingham–Lincoln rail line. Part of it was owned by Coneygre Farm, on the outskirts of the village of Hoveringham, but in the main it was a historic property of Trinity College, Cambridge (Fig 19). Following positive prospecting results, Mr Arnold quickly entered into negotiations with the owners and secured a lease on the land by the end of the year. In early September 1939, production of sand and gravel was underway and Trinity was receiving its first royalty payments. As Mr North wryly remarked, 'For every ton that leaves this quarry, the education of the country benefits (*Newark Advertiser*, 27 October 1954).'

The Hoveringham works was soon exceeding its theoretical maximum capacity of 75 tons per hour, and was profiting from the war boom. The original plant included a 2-foot gauge railway system, on which raw material was hauled for over a mile by two locomotives pulling five trucks holding approximately three tons each. A second internal railway system was used for stripped-off topsoil and overburden, which was tipped back into the worked-out pits. Production was increased by putting more locos and trucks on to the railway system, and working longer hours, so that the plant was soon producing a remarkable 1000 tons of gravel per day, a level that was maintained until 1948. With an old American-built excavator that Arnold had purchased ten years previously, and a workforce of fourteen, the million tons of gravel that the garage proprietor had forecast was dug out by the end of the war. During the war years there were frequent shortages of labour and on occasions the entire plant was being run by a dozen men, with the manager occasionally turning his hand to driving locos. Blackout regulations made work particularly difficult in the winter months

In 1947 Hoveringham Gravel Co was acquired by Harold Needler, a building contractor from Hull, who oversaw the period of the company's most impressive development (Fig 20). After the war he had built up his business interests considerably through the acquisition of local authority housing contracts, on the back of which he purchased some gravel quarries in East Yorkshire. He then learned of the quality of the Hoveringham deposit, and wasted no time in investing in new plant and expanding the business within the Trent Valley. By the mid-1950s the modified plant was producing over 200 tons per hour and, in the words of the quarry manager, 'so far from being just a few holes in the ground, the gravel pit is virtually a self-contained industrial town'. Hoveringham now had 250 employees, most taking advantage of the company's own bus service to get to work. At this time, in addition to the original works at Hoveringham, the company operated quarries at Collingham and Bleasby and had operating agreements at Colwick, Newark and Holme Pierrepont. Dorothy Winn was running the office at Hoveringham Quarry at the time of Harold Needler's takeover of the company:

> There were a lot of changes when Needler took over. He set up a brickworks and a quarry in Canada; he bought a new digger; Noel North brought his brother Emile in who had worked for Needler at Leeds, as a salesman. They took photos for the papers as the new digger was transported down the road. Needler took a half-crown out of his pocket and said 'If that damn thing doesn't pay off, that's all I've got!'

In fact, production records were being broken every year, a feat which sales co-ordinator Emile North attributed to a shrewd understanding of maturing market conditions:

> What we are always concentrating on is the production of first-class aggregate. As the concrete industry, which is now an involved science, progresses, we must always be able to supply just what is wanted. The days when the demand was just for a load of sand and gravel are gone for ever.
>
> (Newark Advertiser, 27 October 1954)

The company was quick to open up new markets. The associated brickworks adjacent to the main premises turned surplus sand into bricks at a rate of up to 90,000 an hour. Two hundred tons of sand were sent to a Leicester tile-making firm in one month and there was a constant coming and going of lorry-loads of material to various parts of the country. Before long consignments of high-quality quartzite gravel were being exported as far afield as Kuwait, India, Malaysia, Singapore and Hong Kong.

By the end of the 1950s the company had also acquired its distinctive logo, a stylised mammoth inspired by an increasing number of fossil finds at the company's quarries and made famous by its appearance on a range of branded toys (Figs 21 and 22). A fleet of company vehicles was assembled in distinctive orange and red livery with matching uniforms for the drivers, inspired by the colours of the chairman's beloved Hull City football team of which he was also chairman. The lorries, predominantly eight-wheeled Fodens, were customised to the company's own specifications and maintained in workshops on the premises. The rapid increase in the size of the vehicle fleet – from 75 in 1954 to 120 three years later – reflected the extraordinary development of the business. The workforce grew from the original fourteen in 1939 to 1,400 employees in 1962 and the company, as the largest aggregates concern in the country, floated on the Stock Exchange in 1963.

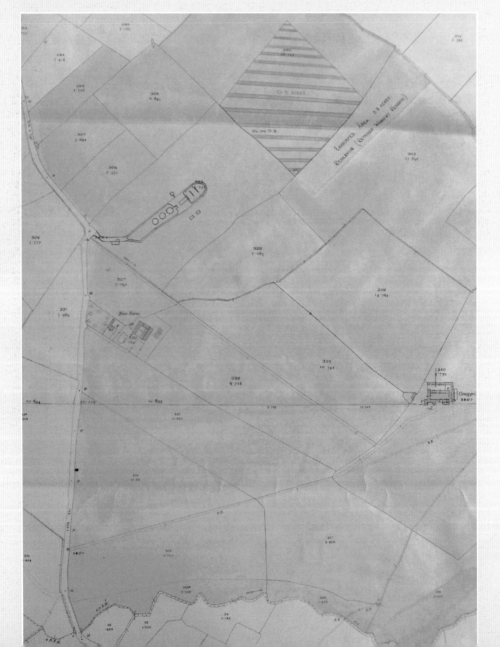

Figure 19
Hoveringham
Quarry in 1947.
Land in yellow
was leased from
Trinity College,
Cambridge, that
in pink from Mr
Buxton of Coneygre
Farm. The strip of
land in blue was
already exhausted
while the area
with grey hatching
was the next to be
worked (Reproduced
by permission of
Nottinghamshire
Archives)

Figure 20 Hoveringham Gravels' chairman Harold Needler, right, shows a mammoth's tusk to the Earl of Bessborough at a publicity event, *c* 1965 (By courtesy of QMJ Publishing Ltd)

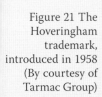

Figure 21 The Hoveringham trademark, introduced in 1958 (By courtesy of Tarmac Group)

Figure 22 Branded model gravel trucks, introduced in the 1960s (Photo: Tim Cooper/ARCUS)

In 1964 the company's holding operation, Needler Developments, bought the Elvaston estate near the Trent in Derbyshire from the earl of Harrington and developed it into one of the largest sand and gravel units in the country. The purchase gave them vast reserves with which to increase their bargaining power and the land was ideally located for transport links using the newly built M1 to serve markets in the increasingly gravel-starved south-east. Rail facilities were installed in the early 1970s to develop further markets outside the Trent Valley. By this time the company had anticipated industry trends by branching out into marine aggregates. More significant had been the development of its ready-mixed concrete subsidiary, which traded under the name of 'Topmix' from over 40 plants throughout the country.

However, by the mid-1970s diversification into related sectors such as leisure and waste disposal could not shield the company from the slump affecting the entire industry. Hoveringham Leisure Ltd initially built successfully on the company's involvement in restoration of old workings into water amenities, such as the acclaimed Country Park at Colwick and the National Watersports Centre at Holme Pierrepont, but the expansion was immediately hit by the energy crisis and three-day week of the early months of 1974. The premature death of Harold Needler in 1975 hastened not only the end of an era in the company's history – indeed, arguably in British industrial history – but the company's demise as an independent concern. The statement issued by the Board of Directors following Mr Needler's death was an accurate assessment of his contribution to the history of aggregates production in the Trent Valley and beyond: 'It was his drive and energy which enabled a small company to grow into the large public company it is today with a pre-eminent position in the aggregate industry.' (Hoveringham Group Ltd, Annual Report 1975) Needler's own philosophy was quite simply stated. The gravel industry, he said, was 'a bit like selling milk: it's consumed from day to day and service and quality are the main ways in which you can compete.' (*Cement Lime and Gravel*, January 1965, p 72) Hoveringham Gravels Ltd, the company whose name he took to the lips of small boys all over the country, was bought by Tarmac Roadstone on the first day of January, 1982.

Note

1. The Trent Valley lies in the East and West Midlands production regions, which produced a combined output of just under 52.5 million tonnes in 2005.

TWO

Process

T he development of sand and gravel working from a local occupation to a
national industry went hand in hand with changes of scale in the type of
site worked, the means of extraction and the conversion of the excavated
material into a marketable product. Already by the 1930s, a range of methods of
both extraction and processing are evident, varying according to local conditions
and requirements (Fig 23).

Preparation

Choice of site

The decision to work a particular deposit is based on a number of considerations
to do with the local geology and topography, prevailing economic conditions
and, inevitably, the need to obtain planning permission. Although sometimes in
conflict, the aspirations of minerals operators and planners have usually been
broadly similar.

Once a potential site had been identified, the primary physical consideration
concerned the projected lifespan of the reserve, as this had the greatest bearing
on the economic viability of the working. The general consensus has been that
a site should provide profitable output for at least fifteen years. The richness
of many Trent Valley deposits has meant that this objective has generally been
met and some sites, such as Attenborough and Hoveringham, have been able to
maintain production considerably longer.

The second most important physical consideration has always been the
ease, or otherwise, of extraction. The main variables here are the level of
the water table and the depth of unusable material ('overburden') overlying
the sand and gravel deposit. Next, the geological composition of the deposit
itself would need to be considered; this is essentially a question of the quality
of the individual sand and gravel components and of the ratio of one to the
other. Operators of 'solid' deposits would also need to ensure that adequate
supplies of water for processing the material could be obtained and that
land was available for site drainage and the positioning of silt lagoons. In
practice, these presented few problems at workings on the valley floor. The
final physical considerations are matters of particular concern to planners:
the means of access from the working area to public roads, the use to which
worked-out pits would eventually be put, and a programme of working that
would enable minimal dereliction of the site.

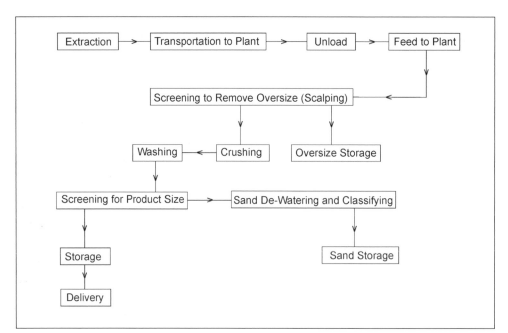

Figure 23 Typical process flow (simplified) for production of sand and gravel aggregates

The main economic consideration is one that is generally shared by both operators and planners; that is, to win the maximum quantity of material in as short a period as possible. More specific to the industry is the need to produce material that will satisfy the anticipated market, and the ability to transport it to market at an acceptable cost. Finally, the prospective operator will need to obtain full planning consent for the site. In addition, if the freehold of the land in question has not been purchased by the operator, arrangements for the payment of royalties need to be made with the landowner.

Borehole testing

The first task to be undertaken once a site had been selected for working was to test the depth of material, and its relation to overburden, throughout the working area. This was done by drilling boreholes, originally by hand with auger and shafts. In the Trent Valley, depths of overburden varied from about half a metre to three metres. Where it was in excess of about 4.5m, working would generally be seen as uneconomic. Similarly, the depth of overburden to productive material could vary considerably, even within the area of a single deposit. Again, this figure (known as the 'overburden ratio') was crucial to decisions about whether, or at least how, to proceed. As a rule of thumb, a ratio in the region of between 1.5 to 2:1 in favour of sand and gravel was sought; below this and working would generally be considered economically unviable. Inevitably, however, as a greater number of sites have been worked, operators have increasingly been prepared to consider shallower deposits.

Borehole testing would also provide an indication of the quality of the material in terms of ease of extraction and processing, strength, and cleanliness. For example, according to Barry Hulland, who worked at a number of Trent Valley sites:

At Hemington it was marvellous material, so clean it was unbelievable. It was only one to two per cent silt and the quality of the material was renowned within the industry. It was very clean and strong.

Removal of overburden

Overburden can be broadly defined as any material overlying the sand and gravel deposit which itself is without direct commercial value (Fig 24). However, its removal is always a significant economic and physical consideration of any aggregates concern. For considerations of removal, it can be further broken down into three distinct layers, or 'horizons'. The first horizon, commonly referred to as topsoil, is biologically active and usually well structured. Below this, the second horizon, or subsoil, is less well structured and biologically less active but plays an important role in the storage of moisture and is essentially topsoil in the making. Modern planning permissions require that topsoil and subsoil are stripped and stored separately in such a way as to maintain their characteristics for later reuse. The third horizon is what is actually referred to as overburden proper and, in the Trent Valley, typically comprises glacial silt or alluvium and often a high content of clayey material.

The earliest gravel pits were uncovered, as at Hilton, simply by men with shovels and a cart. Nor was any great consideration given to the movement or storage of material. Increasingly, however, the priority on-site, both economically and environmentally, has been to minimise the number of times that topsoil and overburden are moved and handled. To the operator it is therefore of great

Figure 24 Sand and gravel deposits below topsoil and overburden, Shardlow Quarry, 2005 (Photo: Tim Cooper/ARCUS)

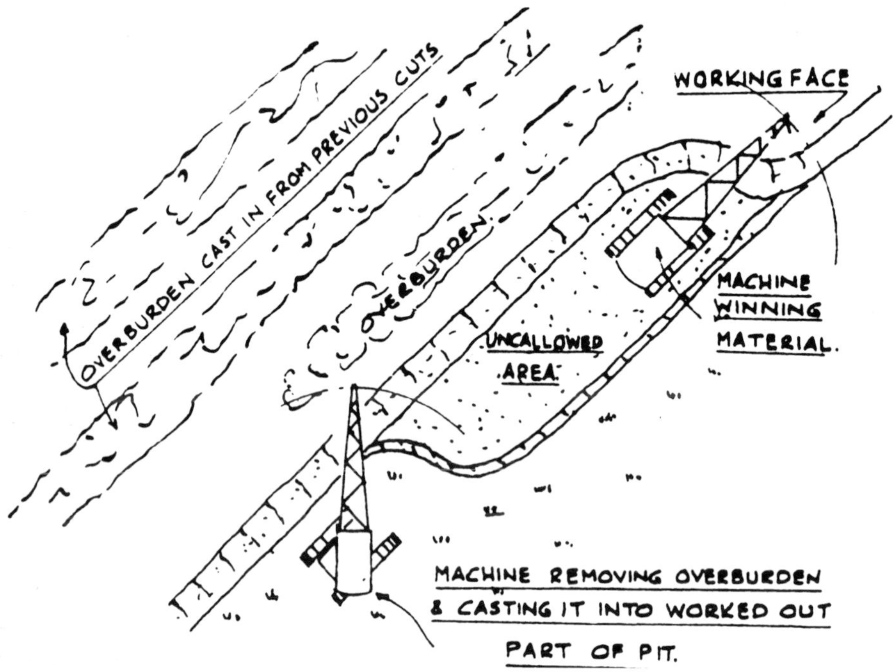

Figure 25
Overburden remova[l]
by 'casting back' (By
courtesy of QMJ
Publishing Ltd)

importance that removal of overburden is fully integrated with the overall plans for the site. This is generally achieved by using overburden for construction and facilitation work such as the building of perimeter banks (known as 'bunds') and the lining or sealing of worked-out areas that are subsequently used for landfill. In some early cases, such work could become a lasting feature of the landscape, such as the flood bank built between the pit at Winthorpe and the nearby village of Holme by 'Lincoln and Hull' following removal of overburden in 1939.

Until the end of the 1950s most overburden removal ('muckshifting' as it is known in the industry) was undertaken by the operating firm itself. However, given the increasing scale of workings, and the requirement for phased excavation and reinstatement of sites, the majority of work now goes out to contract. The type of equipment used for overburden removal has depended on soil-type and the level of the water table, as well as on economic considerations such as the size of the area to be stripped and the distance it has to be carried. Traditionally, the three main methods have been excavation and casting back into a previously worked area, excavation and removal by dumptruck or barge, and mechanical scraping.

Tractor and scraper

Also known as 'tractor and box', this was a common method of overburden removal up to the mid-1950s, particularly on smaller sites such as that operated by Gunthorpe Gravels at that time. A tractor equipped with crawler tracks had the advantage of being able to move well on rough ground but was slower in movement than the wheeled dumpers that came to dominate this part of the process. It also had the advantage that a single operator could perform the various tasks involved, from initial excavation to finishing and contouring of bunds and other earthwork features.

Casting back

This was a popular method up to the 1970s, during the heyday of the dragline excavator and before planning permissions insisted on more stringent soil management schemes. In a simple manoeuvre, the excavator would remove overburden in strips and cast it back onto the floor of the previously worked area (Fig 25). Two operations were thus effectively combined into one, leading to quick and effective excavation. The resulting landscape feature, lagoons containing transverse ridges of overburden, can be seen at sites such as Crankley Point, operated by Hoveringham Gravels Ltd during the 1960s (see Fig 69).

Excavator with dumptrucks or barge

Due to the high volume of overburden in Trent Valley pits from the 1950s onwards the mechanical excavator, either in its dragline or hydraulic form (see below), became the preferred method (Fig 26). Depending on local conditions they might be used either for loading material into barges to be towed away for placing, or with dumptrucks. A variation on this method was the modified boat with an engine and conveyor on top that was used at Girton in the late 1950s. With improvements in dumptruck design, these vehicles became the standard 'muckshifter' and modern overburden removal at Trent Valley sites is almost always an operation carried out by 360° hydraulic excavator and articulated dumptrucks.

Figure 26
Overburden removal with dragline and dumptruck, Girton Quarry, *c* 1956 (By courtesy of Dennis Thacker)

Quarry case study: Trent Concrete Ltd, Colwick, *c* 1922

At this time Trent Concrete operated the largest gravel treatment plant in the country, with a production capacity of 60 tons of crushed and graded aggregate per hour. The unit was operating 24 hours a day, seven days a week, and employed the very latest gyratory crushers which, according to the trade press 'created quite a sensation when they were introduced to this country [from the USA] about two years ago'. As well as conventional vibrating screens for grading material, the plant utilised new automated 'jigging' screens which combined high efficiency with low power consumption.

The plant was housed in a monolithic concrete structure and was thus itself an advertisement for this nascent industry (Fig 27). The production process began with material dredged from the river being brought to a concrete wharf by the dredging boats, from which it was transferred to a primary storage silo by crane grab. From the silos material was discharged as required to a belt conveyor on which it was taken to a rotary screening system (for removal of sand) and then on to the first gravel screen. At this stage, stone material continued on to a primary jaw crusher and then to four screens fitted with jet washers for cleaning. Oversize material proceeded to two roll crushers and the remainder of the material by conveyor to the top of the building for further washing and storage. Adjacent to the plant was a range of spacious workshops in which were produced the company's range of cast concrete products, including window sills, balustrades, tracery windows, and ornamental garden furniture (see Fig 8).

Figure 27 Trent Concrete's Colwick works, *c* 1930 (By courtesy of QMJ Publishing Ltd)

Extraction

The developments that have taken place over time in sand and gravel extraction have been the result of technological adaptation to prevailing geological and environmental conditions. The method employed at any particular pit would need to consider the nature of the deposit (such as its depth and the compactness of material), the height of the water table and the most efficient means of

Figure 28 Suction
pump dredger
in operation at
Attenborough
Quarry, *c* 1930; note
floating pontoons
and housing (By
courtesy of QMJ
Publishing Ltd)

transporting raw material to the processing plant. In the early stages of its development, in particular, the predominant consideration was the height of the water table. As we have seen, early workers of sand and gravel preferred dry pits in the Sherwood Sandstone areas, small-scale riverbank excavation or extraction direct from the river itself. Until the development of high-capacity electric pumps in the 1960s, large-scale exploitation of valley-floor sites would involve working 'wet', that is, taking material from below the water table. So whilst dry pits such as Hilton could employ a mechanical shovel to excavate the face, in the wet pits a variety of methods needed to be employed, including dredging and suction, all of which suffered from the problem of having to excavate material 'unseen'. The consequence on the one hand was that unwanted material such as clay could be included in the load, and on the other that a significant amount of material was lost entirely. Pumping meant that all sites could effectively be worked 'dry', which brought the additional advantage of allowing greater use of electrical machinery such as field conveyors. In modern valley-floor sites the water level is suppressed during the period of operation by a combination of natural and constructed drainage and pumping.

Suction dredgers

In the case of deep deposits with free-running material without too great a quantity of large stones, pumps mounted on pontoons could excavate quite effectively to high capacities. Pumps could either be diesel-powered or electrically operated and could discharge straight to the plant or on to barges. The former method required increases in length of pumping equipment and power consumption as the working area advanced but avoided the need for double-handling of material. Suction pumping was one of the extraction methods employed at Attenborough in the period leading up to the Second World War (Fig 28).

Floating cranes and grabs

Excavators mounted on pontoons or boats were a common method of extraction between the wars, when much material was taken directly from the river or from wet pits (Fig 29). The grab was usually of the clam-shell variety, which could only be used for extracting loose material. A pontoon-mounted grab was one of the

methods used by Trent Gravels at Attenborough in the 1930s and by 'Lincoln and Hull' at Girton up to the mid-1960s. In the latter case they were used particularly during periods of flooding, when land-based excavators were out of action. As with other methods of 'wet' working, the main disadvantage was the inefficiency of working below the water level. Deg Bellamy remembers that when he first went to work at Girton Quarry in the late 1950s:

> They were using very old Priestman excavators, one of them was on a pontoon with a grab. They dug the gravel out of the water, just took the topsoil and the overburden off, and then you'd have water. Everybody did that. They lost thousands of tons of gravel – if you can't see it, you can't get it!

Multibucket ('ladder') dredgers

As described in Chapter 1, these were used extensively, in boat-mounted form, in the river-dredging operations that characterised the early industry in the Trent Valley. They had the advantage over grabs in being able to excavate large volumes of more densely packed material but, conversely, suffered from heavy wear on the chain and bucket apparatus. A ladder dredger designed for Trent Gravels in the mid-1930s was, in the event, not commissioned, since the use of crane-mounted excavators and barges was found to be more economical.

Slackline excavators

Sometimes referred to as 'cable and mast', this method had the advantage of combining the excavation and transport of material to the processing plant with

a minimum of labour and was employed by 'Lincoln and Hull' in their earliest operations at Besthorpe in the 1950s. A bucket attached to a hoist was suspended from a cable running between a steel mast and an anchorage point at ground level. The mast itself was kept in position with the addition of guy lines and the bucket was dropped from the mast into the wet pit, winched up again and its contents deposited into a hopper. Cheap and simple to operate, and especially effective with free-running material, this method had the disadvantage that the bucket would tend to create grooves in the gravel deposit, necessitating fairly frequent movements of the entire apparatus.

Face shovels

In the dry-worked pits of the Trent tributaries, the mechanical shovel or 'navvy' was the principal means of extraction. These were traditionally steam-driven, though some diesel and electric machines were later introduced. They were usually mounted on rails but sometimes on crawler tracks. A steam-operated face shovel was in use at Hilton Quarry during the 1920s and 30s (Fig 30).

Bulldozers

In the Trent Valley area, use of bulldozers was largely restricted to the dry conditions of the Sherwood Sandstone pits, where they were ideally suited to the densely packed material. The usual method of extraction, as practised at Acton (Fig 31), was known as 'rip and doze': a bulldozer fitted with a manganese steel rooter or 'tooth' at the back would effectively plough through the material and then drive back over the same area to use the shovel to break up the material further.

It would then be loaded into field hoppers by an accompanying loading shovel operator. Ken Bagnall carried out 'rip and doze' operations at Acton Quarry:

> You had to be careful working near the face, though there was no danger of it collapsing unless there was blasting going on. There was one area of conglomerate that was so hard you would only work it occasionally once you had exposed it. A manganese steel ripping tooth would only last three-quarters of an hour of continuous ripping but you would work a patch in less time than that and so they would last for a couple of days. A patch would be about 1,500 tons and would take two to three days to process. The ripping teeth and the cutting edges of the dozer were being changed all the time and would cost between £30 and £50 pounds each. If I ripped for an hour I would probably have the rest of the day pushing.

Explosives

Again, in the Trent Valley, blasting was restricted to the Sherwood Sandstone pits. A drilling rig and charges was used in conjunction with excavators in Acton up until the 1970s but was discontinued, for both safety and environmental reasons, to be replaced by 'rip and doze' excavation.

Mechanical excavators

Draglines

The main technological development in sand and gravel extraction in the period leading up to the Second World War was the dragline excavator, which, in the Trent Valley, was to dominate the scene until the introduction of hydraulic machines in the mid-1970s. The most popular machines were those made by Ruston Bucyrus (a part-American-owned subsidiary of the Lincoln firm Ruston & Hornsby) and the Hull-based Priestman company. The Ruston Bucyrus

Figure 31 'Ripping' at Acton Quarry, c 1979 (By courtesy of Bryan Atkin)

excavators (Fig 32) were pneumatically controlled and took their names – for example, 61 RB – from the weight of the machine in tons (later, tonnes), while the Priestmans were controlled by a system of ropes and clutches and sported evocative names such as 'Lion', 'Tiger' and 'Mustang'.

Both types of dragline excavator worked by operating a flattened scoop or bucket attached to a line running along a jib. They required a good deal of skill, usually the result of about six months' training, in operation (see Chapter 4). Tom Dodsley, who started work at Holme Pierrepont Quarry in the early 1970s, describes their use:

Figure 32 Ruston Bucyrus 61 RB dragline excavator at Hoveringham Quarry, *c* 1990 (By courtesy of Tarmac Group)

From an operator's point of view, dragline excavators were a very specialised piece of equipment – a greater number of people can operate hydraulics. The draglines were always having to be adjusted and the drums were controlled by a series of clutches which needed to be altered if, say, the bucket was not stopping in time. Someone driving an excavator without the required skill could do a lot of damage, such as a case we once had of a driver letting a jib go over the back of a machine. It was the most skilled job in the quarry but was always looked on as a team role, because unless it was properly maintained you were not producing anything.

Experienced dragline operators could 'throw' or 'cast' the bucket over a considerable distance, thus winning the greatest amount of material from a single position, though there was always a risk that finer material could be washed out of the bucket. As well as being demanding in terms of learning time, the draglines had a reputation for mechanical solidity and would give years of service before needing to be rebuilt. Indeed, excavation at Hoveringham Quarry was being carried out by a refurbished 61 RB dragline well into the 1990s. Deg Bellamy sums up the affection felt by many in the industry for these machines when he remembers his time at Girton Quarry shortly after it was taken over by Hoveringham Gravels Ltd in the late 1960s:

They bought two Ruston 38 RBs, beautiful machines. They were air-controlled rather than just levers. You had to learn the technique for the old Priestmans – it was about getting a rhythm. The expert driver could take four tons at a time out but he had to make sure it didn't swing about and hit the boat. The Ruston machines were lovely too. When I first went there they had fourteen excavators – you never had to move one! They were old, but they worked.

360° hydraulic excavators

Hydraulically operated extraction equipment, which had become the industry standard in the United States during the 1950s, did not come to the fore in the British market until the late 1970s. From then on they gradually took over in most operating situations, not least because their finger-tip controls were considerably easier to master than the ropes and drums of the old draglines (Fig 33). They also had the advantage of a faster travel speed, meaning that they could cover a greater area of face in a given time and were more effective at other duties, such as overburden stripping, drainage work and earthwork construction.

Figure 33
Caterpillar 360°
hydraulic excavator
at work near Long
Eaton, c 1990 (By
courtesy of Michael
Arthur)

Transportation to plant

With the exception of small-scale workings, and some pits when they were first opened up, transportation of material from working face to processing plant was an integral part of the gravel-winning process. As with the decisions involved in choice of site, the method of transport depended on factors such as local topography, the size of the site and the consistency of the material.

Horse and wagons

Whereas horses and ponies were an indispensable feature of coal mining and stone quarrying for a large part of its history, their use was limited in sand and gravel working because of the wet conditions of river-valley pits. The exception, again, was in the dry pits of the northern Trent tributaries and the Sherwood Sandstone group. Terry Cliff, who went on to work for Hilton Gravel and its successors for a number of years, was first attracted to his local gravel quarry by the sight of horses drawing cartloads of material along the village lanes in the 1940s:

Quarry case study: Trent Gravels Ltd, Attenborough, *c* 1930

In this, the first year of the company's operation, sand and gravel were being excavated from a wet pit adjacent to the Nottingham–Leicester railway line using an 8-inch electric dredger pump mounted on a steel pontoon. The pump delivered material to a box at the top of a dewatering and desanding screen, over which oversize material continued to a large hopper fitted with automatic feeder. This fed back onto six screens of a cantilever design which rejected the larger sizes first and sorted the product into sizes between $3/16$ and $1\frac{1}{2}$ inches. The material was crushed by a combination of rollers and granulators, after which it was stored in overhead bins each with a capacity of about 60 tons. Graded material was then delivered by elevated conveyor across the railway line to bunkers on the other side ready for lorry loading (Fig 34).

Meanwhile, sand and water passed by a chute to a dewatering tank comprising a settling trough containing a bucket elevator which dredged the sand from the water while the overflow ran back to the pond from which the gravel had been extracted. Sand and fine gravel dredged from the dewatering tank was loaded on to railway wagons or stockpiles by means of a five-ton steam-powered grab crane. Following completion in the spring of 1930, the plant regularly maintained close to its maximum capacity of 75 tons of processed material per hour. The pump dredging system remained in place until 1939 when it was replaced by dragline excavators loading a fleet of barges capable of transporting 2000 tons of raw material per day to the plant.

Figure 34 Gravel works straddling the mainline railway at Attenborough, *c* 1930; note railway trucks awaiting loading on sidings to right (By courtesy of QMJ Publishing Ltd)

One of the reasons I used to go to the quarry as a boy was because the gravel was brought up in old-fashioned railway tubs which were pulled by a horse – it was a white horse, I remember it well! The tubs would be filled by steam shovels or draglines. As they moved along the face they would extend the railway line and it would take longer for the horse to pull the tubs. The horse would pull two or three trucks at a time.

By the mid-1950s the horse had been replaced by a small diesel loco, the first driver of which was the man who used to lead the horse. Such was the affection in which the last horse at Hilton was held that upon its retirement the quarry owner, J M Spurrier, insisted that it be allowed to live out its days in his paddock on account of its being 'a good servant to the company'.

Wagons and locos

Before the introduction of field conveyors and all-terrain dumper trucks, these were one of the most widely used methods of internal transport in the sand and gravel industry. As at Hilton, petrol or diesel-powered locomotives frequently replaced horse-drawn or even manually pulled wagons. At the working face, wagons were either fed directly from the excavator or from a feed hopper positioned over the track (Fig 35). The most common form of wagon was the so-called 'Jubilee skip', which Deg Bellamy remembers using at Besthorpe in the early 1960s:

> One crane would be loading into the hopper and another would put one bucketful of wet material straight into each skip. When the crane operator had put a load in each of the skips the train would move under the hopper where somebody would top it up and he would have to make sure it wasn't overloaded, or it couldn't be tipped.

The tipping of the skips into hoppers to feed the main plant required a good deal of strength (the operation is shown in Fig 82). In addition, the operative had to remember always to anchor the skip to the track with a special hook at the top of the hopper, otherwise there was a risk that the axle could break or even that the whole skip would jump from the track. In general, though locos were used for many years in Trent Valley gravel pits, they were never entirely at home in the wet environment and gradually disappeared from the scene around the mid-1960s.

Barge and tug

These were a relatively cost-effective method of internal transportation in a wet pit but required careful co-ordination of operations. During the period when overburden was removed by casting back into the pit it was vital that navigable channels were maintained between the castings. Whilst barges came into their own in the wet conditions of riverside pits, and could remain in use during moderate flooding, they would be put out of action completely in severe winter weather conditions. Both self-powered and dumb barges were used, the latter being either pulled or pushed by small tugs.

At Girton in the 1950s and 1960s material was dug by a combination of draglines and floating grabs and loaded into barges with a capacity of between 80 and 100 tons, which were then towed by tug to a wharf at the processing plant. Here they were unloaded by grabs which discharged into feed hoppers. Workers at the quarry at this time remember how careful the crane drivers had to be not to hit the boat. The operation of the diesel tugs was also seen as a very skilled job, as the drivers needed to avoid the islands of overburden and weave their way carefully to the plant.

Attenborough is the only Trent Valley gravel quarry that has continued to use barges for internal transport up to the present day (the distance from the plant to the working face at Long Eaton is some 4km). Material is loaded into the barges (usually referred to as 'hoppers') by a conveyor belt running from the working face to a loading wharf. The loaded hoppers are then pushed to the processing plant by diesel-powered tugs attached by cables. Bantam tug driver Mick Bugg explains the carefully synchronised loading operation involved:

> When you got to the last bridge you would radio to the man on the wharf to start the feed so that within seconds of getting there the feed would begin. You start loading from the front of the hopper and then keep moving the tug, by letting the rope out that is tied to the wharf, until you are fully loaded. You load by timing in minutes, so you call it an 'eight-minute run-off'. A good load is between 80 and 100 tonnes, depending on the water level. You have to cut down in the dry summer months because the level can drop by about twelve to sixteen inches.

At full capacity, conveyance of material requires co-ordinated use of three tugs on the internal waterway at one time. At the plant end, material is unloaded with a 360° hydraulic loading shovel into a feed hopper. One of the first tasks Assistant Quarry Manager Gary Pell had to master when he arrived at Attenborough was the unloading procedure:

Figure 35 Jubilee wagons, with loco to right, being loaded by dragline and feed hopper, Hoveringham Quarry, *c* 1957 (By courtesy of QMJ Publishing Ltd)

The rhythm of the *three-sixty* is dig/drop, dig/drop, dig/drop. It is quite scary operating them at the wharf so close to the water because you're about ten feet up and you've got about six feet to the water, and then you're dropping about six feet into the boat. By the time that arm is bent over, because your brain is with that arm, you're in the depth of the boat!

Field conveyors

Field conveyors are essentially the same as the conveyor belts used at the plant but employ a modular construction so that they can be extended or reduced in accordance with movements of the working face. They have increased in popularity at Trent Valley sand and gravel pits in line with the development of 'dry' working from the mid-1960s onwards. In addition, the introduction of synthetic materials has meant that conveyors have become more portable and durable. Despite relatively high capital expenditure, both in terms of construction and electricity supply, they are probably the most economical method of internal transport in terms of labour. They become most cost-effective relative to, say, dumper trucks as distance between face and plant increases and/or output rises; their most effective use is in situations where the topography is relatively flat and the shape of the working area keeps movements of the conveyor to a minimum. They are usually fed from the excavator by means of a field hopper positioned across the belt (Fig 36). At Hoveringham Quarry in the early 1990s the combination of a 61 RB dragline excavator and field conveyor was able to transport material over a distance of about 850m at a rate of up to 400 tonnes per hour.

Lorries and dumpers

Where the route between working face and processing plant is relatively dry and easy to maintain, lorries and dumpers provide a straightforward method of internal transport with the advantage of being moved easily between different working faces. Lorry driver Terry Cliff describes this kind of arrangement at Hilton Quarry:

> Because the quarry was not large they started bringing material to the plant by road. They would call that job 'being on the track' because all you did was go down to the face then back to the plant, about 18 or 20 loads a day. They would use mainly contractors on the track and the black and white Hilton lorries would go out on the public roads.

With the development of articulated four- or six-wheeled all-terrain dumptrucks with capacities over 30 tonnes, the need for internal road maintenance decreased; their use was therefore widely adopted (Fig 37). Combined with 360° hydraulic excavators, such vehicles could deliver large quantities of material over relatively long distances and came into their own, compared to field conveyors, when the route between face and plant was over rough ground. At Hemington, excavation was by dragline and dumper by the early 1960s and had the advantage that,

Figure 36 Field
conveyor being
fed by 360°
hydraulic excavator
and field hopper,
Hoveringham
Quarry, 2005
(Photo: Tim Cooper/
ARCUS)

Figure 37 360°
hydraulic excavator
and 6-wheeled
articulated
dumptruck,
Shardlow Quarry,
2005 (Photo: Tim
Cooper/ARCUS)

during the regular periods of flooding, dumpers could be diverted to production from the surge pile (see below). In 2005 Shardlow Quarry was being worked with a 46-tonne 360° hydraulic excavator feeding two 37-tonne articulated six-wheeled dumptrucks. This combination was able to convey material at a rate of more than 300 tonnes per hour over a distance of some 2km between face and plant.

Quarry case study: Hoveringham Gravels Ltd, Hoveringham, *c* 1957

Unlike the previous two examples, the main plant components at Hoveringham were manufactured on-site in the company's workshops. At this time the deposit was worked 'wet', the water table lying at a level of about one metre below the ground surface. Excavation was by 38 RB and 54 RB draglines loading into field hoppers constructed astride a 2-foot gauge railway track (see Fig 35). This arrangement fed tipping wagons hauled six at a time by two Ruston and Hornsby four-cylinder diesel locomotives delivering a combined load of 18 tons of material on each trip to the plant. The railway track, of 'Jubilee' type, consisted of main and branch line sections running up to two working faces, which could be moved or extended as required. At this time the distance from face to plant varied between a quarter of a mile and one mile. On arrival at the plant the wagons discharged at two 30-ton steel receiving hoppers installed below track level. The wagons were tipped by hand to discharge into the hoppers (see Fig 82), from which the material initially passed over a five-inch scalping screen (see below) for removal of cobbles. Material then passed into a second hopper and was fed to the plant conveyors via a vibrating chute. Normal input to the plant was 240 tons of material per hour (Fig 38).

The material was processed at three plants, Nos 1 and 2 being designed to operate independently, while No. 3 drew material from either of the first two following separation of sand and 'oversize'. No. 3 plant could also be fed with crushed material which went to separate storage bins. Material was taken from Nos 1 and 2 to rotary washers via 24-inch inclined conveyors. All sand and oversize was removed by the washers, after which the sand passed with the wash water to a collection tank for further agitation and pumping by a Linatex vortex-type sand pump (see below) to the sand classifying tower. Here the water was extracted and allowed to flow away with fines to an exhausted part of the quarry while the sand passed from the bottom of the Linatex cones to form a large stock pile on the concrete floor below. It was then transferred by drag-bucket and scrapers to two storage hoppers to await lorry-loading. By this method the sand was drained of virtually all surplus water before being placed in the hoppers. Special fine sand for tile-making could be produced by means of a second jacket fitted into the washer of the No. 1 plant.

Rejects from the two horizontal screens, ie material of +1.5 inches, were sorted for feeding either directly into lorries or choke-fed into a 24-inch cone crusher.

Before reaching the final conveyor feeding the hoppers, material was given further washing by means of a reciprocating-type screen. Water for the various washing processes was pumped from a lagoon in an exhausted part of the quarry near the plant.

Storage was in 20 bins, each with a capacity of 100 tons. These were of steel frame construction with renewable timber partitions, and gravel was manually discharged through doors beneath, first passing over a static screen for a final wash before being loaded into lorries. Product was weighed prior to delivery on two Pooley weighbridges.

Figure 38 Main feed to plant at Hoveringham Quarry, 1957 (By courtesy of QMJ Publishing Ltd)

Processing

Plant design

Despite the fact that over time, and from site to site, there has been some variation in the design and layout of sand and gravel processing plant, it has all carried out the same essential functions: washing the material and then separating it into different particle sizes to meet customer requirements. Once geologists have satisfied potential operators as to the size and quantity of available material, plant designers or materials handling engineers are then employed to envision

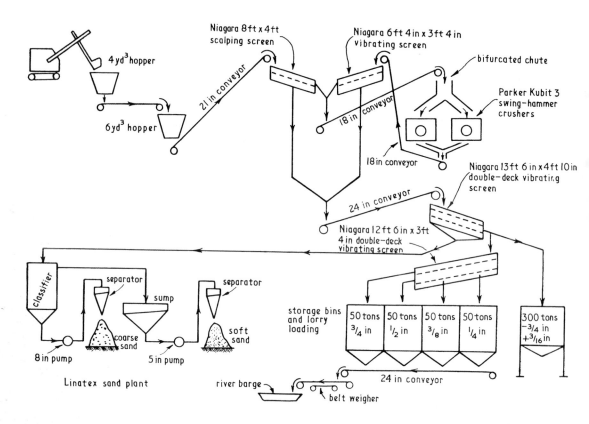

the process of conveying raw material through various cleaning and screening areas to the final point of sale. This has traditionally been done by means of a flow diagram showing the quantity and type of material passing through each section of the plant, as well as indicating the direction of material flow, in a similar form to that of electrical circuit diagrams (Fig 39).

Figure 39 Flow diagram for new plant at Meering, 1969 (By courtesy of QMJ Publishing Ltd)

Ideally, operators would want new plant to be positioned as near as possible to the centre of the working area, if this was extensive, but preferably in a non-productive area; they would want it on a part of the site that had good drainage and they would want sufficient space around it to ensure safe access and ease of maintenance. If a new plant was being designed at an existing site they would want it positioned in an area that had already been worked. All plants require good access to public roads. Planners will share some of the same objectives as operators and, in addition, will want the plant to keep the lowest possible profile, both literally and figuratively in terms of its impact on the local environment.

Unloading and feeding

Unloading can be defined as the transfer of raw material from internal transport to the processing system, and feeding as the control of the rate of flow of the material from one stage of the process to another. In early stages of industrial development, or at smaller pits, material was sometimes unloaded directly to

Figure 40 Main feed to plant at Hoveringham Quarry, 2005. Note primary stockpile conveyor to rear discharging to surge pile over recovery tunnel from which recovery conveyor transports material into plant at front of picture (Photo: Tim Cooper/ARCUS)

the plant, for example from field conveyors or by dumptrucks unloading into a receiving hopper. The latter was the method employed at Gunthorpe Gravels' quarry, where material excavated by 22 RB dragline was dumped at the top of a tipping ramp. At larger workings, and almost universally over time, a 'surge pile' was employed in the form of a buffer stock of unprocessed material waiting to be fed into the processing plant. The benefit of this system was that it enabled consistently high-capacity production through use of the surge pile during stoppages either at the face or the unloading stage.

The most common method of providing surge capacity is a naturally forming conical stockpile built up over one or two conveyor belts ('reclaim feeders') positioned in a tunnel below (Fig 40). Material is unloaded to a feed hopper which introduces it to the processing plant at a consistent rate via a conical chute. Material which flows by gravity into the chute is referred to as the 'live' feed, whilst that left at the side is 'dead' stock, which must be gradually moved to a 'live' position, usually by a loading shovel. Within the plant, material is transported from one processing stage to another by conveyors. Traditional rubber and canvas conveyors have gradually been superseded by belts made of synthetic materials and those above ground level are fitted with walkways and handrails to facilitate safe maintenance.

Screening

This is the process by which material is separated into different sizes by being passed over perforated decks (screens) (Fig 41). Traditionally, screening has been further divided into the stages of 'scalping', a preliminary stage which removes oversize material, often including balls of clay, either for crushing or outright rejection; 'sizing', in which material is separated into different sizes or 'products'; and 'dewatering', which is a stage in the removal of excess water from

Figure 41
Screening of totally crushed gravel at Hoveringham, 2005
(Photo: Tim Cooper ARCUS

the material. The most common form of processing screens is of a mechanically vibrating type, with a number of decks sometimes being mounted in a single vibrating frame. As in conveying, older steel screens are gradually being replaced by synthetic compounds, particularly polyurethane, which sacrifice some efficiency for considerably greater durability and ease of maintenance.

In normal procedure, up to three different products are made from a single screen by means of multiple decking. In a two-deck screen, for example, material passing over the top deck will constitute one product while that passing through is divided into two more by the deck below. Both sizing and dewatering screens can be used for final rinsing by the fitting of water jets. The aim of the primary screening process is to 'top and tail' the feed, meaning the removal of the largest material (usually somewhere between +75mm and +40mm) and that below 5mm, in other words sand. Oversize gravel will then overflow the upper deck

Figure 42 Cone crusher at Attenborough Quarry, 2005 Photo: Tim Cooper/ ARCUS)

of the screens, usually for crushing and subsequent reintroduction, and the sand proceeds with wash water to the lower decks. Further screening then takes place according to the product capabilities of the particular site. A typical 4/20 concreting mix is made by recombining different sizes that have been separately screened.

Crushing

The conversion of raw material into a range of different products is assisted by the process of mechanical crushing. Unlike stone, gravel as quarried already comes in various sizes and crushing is mainly applicable to the fraction between 40mm and 20mm. Indeed, too much crushed material in a concreting aggregate can lead to a reduction in strength. The crushing process is often divided into two distinct phases: 'primary', which reduces large material such as cobbles, and 'secondary', in which material in the +50mm size range is reduced further. In gravel processing, two different types of mechanical crusher have traditionally been employed: gyratory or cone crushers, and impact crushers. Jaw crushers, used extensively in stone quarries, have little use except in reducing exceptionally large reject material.

Gyratory and cone crushers essentially employ the same mechanical action but the cone has a differently shaped crushing chamber. Cone crushers are mechanically very robust and are therefore widely used on all common size reductions (Fig 42). Impact crushers work by the material being simultaneously thrown against a fixed surface and accelerating outwards from a spinning concentric shaft. In the variation known as the 'hammer mill', material fed into the top is struck by rotating hammers and thrown against stationary 'breaker' plates made from manganese steel. The hammers may be either rigidly fixed or free to swing on pivots. In terms of abrasion, gravel is very hard on crushers, with hammer mills particularly requiring frequent replacement of parts. The hammers used in the machinery at Girton in the 1960s, for example, would only last about a week. Over time, due to their greater durability, cone crushers were universally adopted at sand and gravel plants throughout the Trent Valley.

Washing

The purpose of washing plant is to convert an excavated mass of gravel, sand, clay, silt and other deleterious materials into a saleable product. Gravel mixed with clay particles is usually cleaned by passing through one or more agitating washing barrels (or 'scrubber mills') containing water, whilst fine silt or clay particles can be removed by high-pressure jets of water directed at the material as it passes over screens (Fig 43). Silt that is washed out during processing is left to settle in specially designated ponds. Different sites are variously affected by the presence of contaminants in the sand and gravel as dug. The most common in river-valley deposits is lignite (or 'brown coal') which, if allowed to remain with the aggregate, disintegrates and leads to surface staining. Increasingly sophisticated equipment has been developed for the removal of lignite, though all essentially works on the principle that it is less dense than the sand from which it is eventually extracted. Before the introduction of a Floatex lignite separating plant at Repton, a site that particularly suffered from this type of contamination, the material was manually removed and was not entirely unwanted:

> It was all hand-picked off the belts and the farmers used to fetch it in loads and burn it on the old Aga stoves – it used to burn with a tremendous heat! (Barry Hulland)

Sand dewatering and classification

Dewatering refers to the process of reducing the moisture content in sand, and classification to the grading of sand to comply with specification requirements. In practice, the two processes are often combined. Sand that is to be used for concrete manufacture is almost always washed to reduce the silt content that can compromise durability. Early dewatering equipment, such as that installed at Attenborough in 1929, comprised a tank into which the slurry of small material passed; water simply overflowed the top while the sand that settled at the bottom was recovered by a chain-driven bucket elevator.

More sophisticated sand plant, first introduced in the 1950s, was designed to carry out the multiple tasks of de-watering, silt removal, and classification. The first stage of the modern process is usually the dewatering of slurries on high-frequency vibrating screens, most recently of a modular polyurethane construction for maximum resistance to wear and ease of maintenance. Fine material collected from these washing screens is then passed to a settling tank which removes silt while commencing the process of grading.

Final classification is usually by means of a 'hydrocyclone' unit in which opposing centrifugal forces, and those of an inward-acting drag, accelerate the settling rate of particles and separate them according to size (Fig 44). Faster-settling particles move to the wall of the cyclone and exit at the bottom (apex) while the action of the drag force moves slower-settling particles into a spiral of low pressure at the centre by which they are carried upwards to exit at the

Figure 43 Plant at Attenborough, *c* 1965, showing scrubber barrel in foreground; note barges and grab crane at wharf below (By courtesy of Cemex UK)

overflow. The exact classification obtained is tailored to the particular needs of the quarry by adjusting variables including the diameter of the cyclone and the apex and the amount of pressure drop achieved within the unit.

Water supply and management

It will be seen from the above that one of the essential requirements of a sand and gravel plant is an adequate supply of clean water for washing. Other than obtaining the required licences from the water authorities, this does not usually present a problem at the terrace deposits, but can require more planning in the case of those in the Sherwood Sandstone group. Most water supply schemes combine the installation of pumping equipment with the use of natural watercourses, such as that employed at Shardlow from 2003 which involved pumping from Aston Brook and temporary drains to the processing plant, circulation through the site's lagoon system, and discharge into the Trent.

Silt lagoons, or settling ponds for the reception of water from the washing units, usually make use of old workings close to the plant, also helping to reduce the cost of pumping clean surface water back into the washing system. Generally, the amount of surface water generated at sand and gravel plants due to stockpile drainage, spillage and so on is usually too great for the ground to absorb and additional drainage needs to be installed. In its simplest form, such as employed at Acton Quarry in the Sherwood Sandstone group, this entails ensuring that wherever plant is positioned excess water can drain to the lowest part of the site.

Figure 44
Dewatering cyclone mounted on radially traversing gantry discharging to sand stockpile, Shardlow Quarry, 2005. Note semicircular track of gantry allowing movement of stockpiling position (Photo: Anna Badcock/ARCUS)

Figure 45 Product
stockpiles formed by
overflow conveyors
at Shardlow Quarry,
2005 (Photo: Tim
Cooper/ARCUS)

Product storage

At all sites, irrespective of size, some form of storage is required, mainly for processed sand and gravel but occasionally for raw material awaiting processing. Traditionally, storage has been in the form of hoppers, sometimes built directly under the processing plant itself and constructed of wood, steel, or concrete. The bottom of above-ground hoppers would normally be in conical form to ensure complete discharge of material.

In more recent years there has been a gradual move away from the use of hopper storage due to their relatively limited capacity and height restrictions on plant universally imposed by planning permissions. Ground-level stockpiles of sand and gravel are usually formed at the end of conveyors and assume conical form (Fig 45), or in heaps as formed by mechanical loading shovels. More discreet forms of storage include concrete bays or 'toast racks' used in the early plant at Hoveringham, or timber-framed sand storage areas, as at Attenborough. Ground storage also has economic advantages and is a popular option at quarries with limited reserves and therefore a shorter lifespan. Sand can be particularly difficult to discharge from hoppers and ground storage also allows for continuing drainage. Washed sand is almost always stocked on the ground directly following discharge from hydrocyclones, dewatering towers or low-incline conveyors.

Process control

The most significant innovation in sand and gravel production since the Second World War has been the automation of the production process and its control from a single remote point (Fig 46). Typically, individual components of process control systems will include sequencing equipment, belt weighers, closed circuit television (CCTV) monitoring and metal detection. Sequencing control involves co-ordinating the commencement of individual stages in production, such as screens, conveyors and crushers, to occur only when equipment at a later stage is already functioning. This is done mainly to avoid possible blocking of downstream plant; the most obvious example would be the requirement in a series of field conveyors for the last to be started first and the feeder belt last.

Belt weighers are used to monitor throughput and production levels. Load-cells located on individual idlers on the conveyors feed back data in digital form for both continuous and staged monitoring. Typical use would be the monitoring of plant efficiency through comparisons of daily tonnages. The main application of CCTV is for real-time monitoring of crucial stages in the process that are otherwise relatively inaccessible. A typical example would be to check high-level conveyors for possible overloading. Metal detectors installed over the main recovery conveyor help to avoid stray metal objects (such as broken pieces of mobile plant) from damaging the plant and, incidentally, occasionally lead to the identification of archaeological artefacts.

Many modern plants, such as that built at Girton in 2004, are regulated by a computerised system known as Programmable Logic Control (PLC) which is essentially a more sophisticated system of sequence control. The upgrading of equipment at Shardlow in 2006, for example, was able to provide closer monitoring of product grades, a more logical sequencing system and higher-level reporting of performance data.

Product loading and delivery

The final stage in the sand and gravel production process involves the loading of material into vehicles. The earliest mechanical systems, such as that in use at Hoveringham in the 1950s, released material from overhead hoppers into the back of the lorry by the simple pull of a chain by the driver. The volume of sale would then be ascertained by reading a mechanical dial at the weighbridge. By the 1970s, many quarries, such as Repton and Shardlow, had introduced automatic systems comprising overhead conveyors with feed regulated directly by load-cells incorporated in the weighbridge. A number of plants, including Hoveringham up to the point of closure, continued to load vehicles straight from ground-level stockpiles with mechanical loading shovels.

By the early 1980s more sophisticated weighbridge systems were being introduced which included automatic printing of dispatch tickets and CCTV monitoring. At the modern Shardlow Quarry, orders are printed from the control centre computer on a daily basis and logged by the weighbridge clerk. Vehicles arriving on site are allocated to the relevant order and, after automatic loading

Figure 46 Interior of control building at Shardlow Quarry, 2005. Note monitoring of plant operation to left with controllers for crushers to right and CCTV monitors to far right (Photo: Anna Badcock/ARCUS)

in the yard, the driver is given a conveyance ticket in duplicate which is checked and signed before departure. The computer system identifies any apparently erroneous vehicle and loading actions and is able to keep track of vehicle movements following departure.

Ready-mixed concrete plant

Some quarries in the Trent Valley developed a close association between the processes of sand and gravel production and ready-mixed concrete at an early stage, and incorporated specialist plant accordingly. By the end of the 1950s there were already significant variations in the mechanics of concrete delivery, from simple manual control to highly automated push-button plants. The essential requirement of any plant, however, was the ability to weigh every ingredient accurately.

At the Attenborough works of Trent Gravels Ltd, one of the pioneers in the field, the original batching plant was designed so that grading of aggregates and batching of mixes was done by dry weight. Instrumentation controlled the quantity of water present in the aggregates and a series of bins at the top of the plant provided a choice of up to five different sizes of aggregate and sand according to the grading required. The company started with a fleet of Jaeger truck mixers, each with a capacity of 2.5 cubic yards. The aggregates and cement were loaded into the drum of the mixer and the required quantity of water for mixing was carried in a separate tank. This allowed dry mixing if required, or, alternatively, the water could be introduced during transport or on arrival at the job.

At an early stage, a fully equipped laboratory was built at the quarry in which aggregates were tested for silt content and organic matter and concrete-setting and compression tests were made according to British Standards. Aggregate was supplied to the batching plant by belt conveyor from the gravel plant while bulk cement deliveries were handled by a pump, not unlike a domestic vacuum cleaner, which raised cement from ground-level storage to bins above the weighing floor of the plant. By the early 1960s the company had a fleet of 22 truck mixers, and the huge increase in public works projects at that time saw the introduction of larger-capacity high-discharge vehicles.

Quarry case study: Douglas Aggregates Ltd, Barton-under-Needwood, *c* 1979

In the late 1970s Douglas Concrete and Aggregates Ltd was working a substantial deposit of river terrace gravel at Barton-under-Needwood near Burton upon Trent. The Douglas Group was at the time involved in a number of major construction projects in the Midlands, including the National Exhibition Centre near Birmingham, the M42, and a number of other motorway, local authority, industrial, and commercial contracts. The aggregates division was mainly concerned with the production and sale of ready-mixed concrete for which the bulk of the raw material was supplied by the Newbold gravel pit just outside the village of Barton.

The site had first been developed for aggregate production by the company in 1963 when a washing and screening plant was installed to process 80 tons of material per hour. This was replaced in the late 1970s by a new plant with an increased capacity of 250 tons per hour (Fig 47). A major consideration of the design of the new plant was that it should be ahead of the prevailing planning conditions by fitting as closely and as inconspicuously as possible into its local environment. The innovative washing and screening plant was totally enclosed in a single building designed to be less visually obtrusive than conventional arrangements. It also protected both plant and employees from the elements and allowed repairs to be carried out in any weather and at any time of the day or night.

The gravel deposit lay mainly below the water table and was overlain by about 1m of overburden and 30cm of topsoil which was stripped by tractor and scraper and stockpiled ready for replacement following back-filling of the worked-out area with pulverised fuel ash (PFA) pumped from nearby Drakelow power station. The pit was worked by a 71 RB dragline loading onto a 600-yard field conveyor system via a feed hopper with a capacity of 250 tons per hour. This carried material 'as dug' to a raw material stockpile of 3000 tons' live capacity formed over a recovery tunnel. No storage bins were required since the plant produced only two grades of gravel – 20mm and 10mm – which were separately stockpiled over the reclaim tunnel.

The washing and screening plant was fed by two vibrating feeders under the raw material stockpile that discharged onto a reclaim conveyor, which in turn discharged onto the main plant feed conveyor. A triple-decker vibrating screen equipped with spray bars and fitted with meshes of 25mm, 12mm, and 6mm removed the sand and passed the gravel to a scrubber. This was followed by a horizontal double-deck vibrating screen also fitted with spray bars which graded the gravel into the two product sizes of 20mm and 10mm, plus oversize. The product sizes were taken by two conveyors to separate product stockpiles, each with a capacity of 3000 tons. The oversize that came off the end of the screen was taken by conveyor to a surge hopper of 1000 tons' capacity mounted over two cone crushers, one of which was fitted with variable speed control. Once reduced, the material was then returned in close circuit by another conveyor for further screening. Sand and water were carried away by flumes fitted beneath a scrubber barrel and the screens to a pair of sumps; from these the sand was then pumped up to two Linatex sand separators, from which it formed a stockpile.

The gravel stockpiles were formed over a single reclaim tunnel on top of a conveyor belt fed by four paddle blenders, two for each grade. This discharged to a lorry-loading belt with a loading capacity of four tons per minute. The lorry-loading was controlled, and single-sized or blended material delivered as required, from the weighbridge office, the weighbridge itself being a 30-ton unit with a 10m platform. All delivery from the quarry was by the Douglas Group's fleet of 24-ton and 30-ton Leyland vehicles. Truck mixers operating from the site, also owned by the company, were Thompson units on a Leyland Bison chassis. All vehicles were maintained at the on-site workshop and a separate workshop took care of the processing plant.

Figure 47 Artist's conception for new plant at Barton-under-Needwood, *c* 1979 (By courtesy of QMJ Publishing Ltd)

Transportation to market
River and rail

In the period up to the early 1950s, when large volumes of sand and gravel in the Trent Valley were being dug from the bed of the River Trent itself, it was inevitable that markets would develop along the communication lines provided by the rivers; that is, via the Humber to Hull and Grimsby, and the canal from Torksey to Lincoln. By the mid-20th century quite significant bulk trade had developed on the Trent. This included barges belonging to 'Lincoln and Hull' taking gravel from the riverside works at Girton for processing at Hull and returning with loads of sugar, flour and, increasingly, phosphate fertiliser for loading onto smaller boats at Torksey for transfer by canal to the Fisons plant at Saxilby. The imported cane sugar market often involved Trent 'gravellers' taking supplies from Hull up the River Ouse to the Yorkshire markets of Selby, Castleford and Leeds before returning up the Trent for further supplies of gravel.

Jetties for receiving barges had been built by 'Lincoln and Hull' at Winthorpe and Besthorpe pits soon after they were opened in 1939, and subsequently at Girton in 1950. Material was loaded as raw ballast from Winthorpe and sent in the company's own barges to Hull for processing; most of the barges were steam-powered, though a few ran on diesel. Once processed in Hull, material was sent mainly to markets in East Yorkshire. At Besthorpe and Winthorpe processed material was loaded onto barges, either by conveyor or lorry, with delivery of loads being taken on the basis of the individual boat's draught (Fig 48). The quarry had a chart of the capacities of the various barges and, where different material was loaded fore and aft, a calculation based on mean draft was used. Deg Bellamy was a foreman at Besthorpe in the 1960s:

> The barges were all different sizes, anything from 100 tons to 600. The little ones were used on the canals where it wasn't so deep. They used to come when the [coal] miners had their holidays, because they usually carried coal and then they would have nothing to do for a fortnight so they fetched gravel.

Barges would leave Hull with written orders for the quantities and type of material that was required. They came and went with the tide, on the upriver journey mainly to save fuel, on the return to make sure they could actually make it with a full load. Dependence on the tides meant that boats might visit the quarry during the night, in which case, at Girton, crews would load the craft themselves from the hoppers and leave a note as to the type and quantity of material they had taken. During the day the processing plant at Hull would sometimes phone the quarry to amend orders for boats that were on their way, according to changes in sales. Most of the barges would leave Hull as soon as the tide started to rise and would normally get as far upriver as Marnham or Laneham before the water was too low for further progress. There they would wait for the next tide – boatmen would call it waiting until you 'made it' – which could be twelve hours, or more during the low-water periods of summer months. Only on occasions when there was a lot of flood water were fully loaded boats able to make it back to Hull in one go. As well as to Hull, smaller boats would

Figure 48 Belt feeding of barge at Besthorpe wharf, c 1969 (By courtesy of QMJ Publishing Ltd)

be used to take material to a distribution depot in Newark, from which it would be carried by road.

The disadvantages of barge haulage for the sand and gravel industry had already been recognised by the Waters Committee as early as 1946; not only was it dependent on the tides but return loads of produce were becoming increasingly difficult to source. More than anything, however, the river traffic was hampered by the economic disadvantage of double-handling. A slight change in haulage economics in the early 21st century saw the Lafarge company reintroduce barge shipment from Besthorpe to the newly opened Europort near Wakefield in West Yorkshire. Otherwise, Deg Bellamy sums up the demise of this period in the industry's history succinctly:

> With barges it all had to be handled two or three times. They used to send hundreds of thousands of tons of gravel to Hull and Grimsby; I've seen fifteen or twenty boats waiting for gravel. They had to wait while they 'made it' – they might be waiting for a couple of days.

Rail transport was perhaps never likely to become of great significance to an industry producing a low-value bulk product for which handling costs were prohibitive; movements of more than about 20 miles were generally considered to double ex-pit price. Ironically, those operators working quarries particularly close to railway lines, such as Hoveringham and Trent Gravels, were the first to introduce their own haulage fleets. The economic disadvantages were compounded by the rationalisation of the railway network in the early 1960s and the adoption of single-load trains a little later.

So universal was the move towards road haulage that in 1964 the board of British Railways wrote to government ministers making the case for increased use of their facilities for the transport of sand and gravel, offering inducements such as the use of recently decommissioned yards as ready-mixed concrete depots. However, by this time the future pattern of aggregates haulage had been established and, indeed, Trent Gravels at Attenborough was one of the companies to have already had its own sidings removed.

Road transport and long-range markets

As supplies of river-dredged gravel neared exhaustion, and exploitation of the river terraces coincided with developments in motor vehicles, road transport increasingly became the norm, a trend that was already apparent at the outbreak of the Second World War. However, post-war legislation, such as the introduction of a 44-hour working week and a new licensing system, together with wage increases across the haulage sector, had an immediate impact on the distance that material could be economically conveyed. Despite a special agreement reached in 1947 between the sand and gravel industry and the Road Haulage Association for special rates to apply to deliveries to East Coast markets such as Grimsby, economic forces inevitably hastened the decline of production from pits in the 'Lincolnshire Triangle' and an assumption of their former dominance by the new, larger quarries on the Nottinghamshire Terraces. By the early 1950s, increased levels of taxation and the higher cost of fuel had led to further increases in the cost of distribution, prompting operators into decisions about whether to continue using contractors or to set up their own vehicle fleets.

Figure 49 New vehicle fleet, with drivers in company livery, Hoveringham Quarry, c 1948. Compare main plant in background with Fig 80 (By courtesy of Nigel Hunt)

Figure 50
Hoveringham
Gravels' driver
Raymond Hunt
with Dodge truck,
c 1957. Such vehicles
featured in the
film *Hell Drivers*,
released in the same
year (By courtesy of
Nigel Hunt)

In fact, Hoveringham Gravels had already started assembling its own fleet in the spring of 1948, when it took delivery of a number of Ford Thames tippers in the company's distinctive orange and red livery (Fig 49). Later that year, further additions of four- and six-wheeled Albion and eight-wheeled Foden vehicles were made. The garage facilities at Hoveringham Quarry were enlarged accordingly and, following purchase of a number of new Dodge trucks, in 1954 the company had a fleet of no fewer than 75 delivery vehicles built to its own safety specifications. In response to a question concerning his aspirations for his runaway business, Hoveringham chairman Harold Needler was widely reported as saying 'A hundred quarries and a thousand lorries.'

These were heady days for the gravel industry, reflected by the 1957 film *Hell Drivers* in which a star cast (including a debut by future James Bond Sean Connery) played the roles of gravel truck drivers racing full-throttle around the English countryside, literally stopping at nothing to take the prize for greatest number of daily deliveries. Whether or not, as some have claimed, the film's gritty realism was inspired by the antics of Hoveringham drivers (and given the company's impressive safety record, that is perhaps unlikely) gravel companies were undoubtedly providing incentives for their drivers to reduce delivery times (Fig 50). All the main Trent Valley gravel companies had their own fleets of vehicles by the mid-1960s and some, such as Trent Gravels and Hilton Gravel, were doing their best to compete with Hoveringham in the visibility stakes (Fig 51). Hilton, for example, used unmarked contract vehicles on its internal trips between quarries and plant while the black-and-white liveried Bedford trucks were reserved for use on public roads. This was a time when small boys up and down the country counted their model Hoveringham tipper truck among their favourite toys (see Fig 22).

It was, indeed, quite appropriate that it should be a Trent Valley company's vehicles that featured in their games. Increasingly, the bold predictions of the Hoveringham chairman were coming true, with local firms supplying ever more distant markets. By the 1960s, not only the larger companies, but smaller long-established operators such as Robert Teal Ltd of Carlton-on-Trent, had found markets for specialist material as far afield as Hong Kong, Singapore, Malaysia, Mauritius, India, Libya, Brazil, and the Falkland Islands. The fine Hoveringham gravel used in water filtration plants in Kuwait made a significant contribution to that country's economic development until their destruction by Saddam Hussein's forces in the first Gulf War (1990).

Back at home, large-scale redundancies in the 1980s forced a significant change on the haulage component of the industry, which since then has operated mainly on an owner/driver basis. In the early 21st century, drivers working for Hanson Aggregates, for example, obtained financial assistance to buy their vehicles and were given guaranteed work for a period of four years to enable them to pay off the loan. Increasingly, companies became involved in joint schemes, such as that negotiated between Hanson and Tarmac in the 1990s.

Figure 51 Trent Gravels lorries, *c* 1965 (By courtesy of Michael Arthur)

Quarry case study: ARC Aggregates Ltd, Shardlow, *c* 1992

Figure 52 Main processing plant at Shardlow Quarry, 2005. From left to right, primary crusher; twin outlet feeders to main processing plant in centre with ground stockpiles of various products below; final screening section and storage hoppers (Photo: Tim Cooper/ ARCUS)

A new high-capacity plant, capable of producing 1 million tonnes a year, was installed at Shardlow Quarry by the then owner, ARC Central, in 1992. A key element was an environmentally sensitive buildings design, with all main components clad in light-coloured panels to minimise the plant's impact as seen against the sky (Fig 52). The plant incorporated many state-of-the-art features, including a new lignite removal process, metal detection, belt weighing and a centralised PLC control point. To facilitate maintenance and reduce costs, all screen decks comprised polyurethane modules and all plant cladding was made of plastic-coated sheeting. In addition, all machinery was provided with suitable lifting beams and joists to facilitate removal and maintenance. A noticeable safety feature of the plant when compared with many earlier examples was the provision of generous access platforms and 45° walkways throughout.

The deposits on site were up to 10m deep, with an average depth of 5m, and overlay Triassic Mercia Mudstone. The average grading of material was 64% gravel, 33% sand, and 3% silt and clay, with an overburden of soils and clayey alluvium. The water table was generally at a high level in the sand and gravel horizon. Overburden was removed by contractors using hydraulic excavators and high-capacity dumptrucks. Raw material was extracted by hydraulic 360° excavator that fed two 40-tonne capacity articulated dumptrucks which discharged over a reject grid into an 80-tonne capacity reception hopper. Positioned below this in a reclaim tunnel was a vibrating-tray feeder regulating feed to a primary stockpile (or surge pile) conveyor equipped with twin rotating plough units for the removal of oversize lumps of clay and rock.

The surge pile had a live capacity of 2500 tonnes, providing regular feed of 450 tonnes per hour to the processing plant. Mounted in a second tunnel beneath, twin vibrating-tray feeders delivered to a recovery conveyor discharging to a splitter hopper with twin outlet feeders which divided the material into two equal lines of feed to the first processing section. Each of these lines comprised a double-deck vibrating screen which rejected the +150mm material to ground storage, selected the -150mm/+40mm fraction for crushing and passed the -40mm on for lignite removal.

The primary crusher was of cone type which cut in and out automatically as required, in response to special probes within its feed hopper. The crushed product was returned in closed circuit with one of the primary screens, the other being reserved for uncrushed material so that a range of natural gravels could be produced. The PLC ensured that both sides of the plant received equal feed at all times irrespective of whether the crusher was in operation. The -40mm material which passed over the lower deck was conveyed to a gravel deligniting station in which any -40mm/+5mm lignite and other low-density contaminates were floated out, leaving clean gravel to discharge directly to two low-angle triple-deck vibrating screens for washing and grading.

The secondary crusher comprised one cone unit that received the -40mm/+20mm fraction and another which received surplus -20mm/+10mm material. Both units discharged to a common conveyor which returned the product in closed circuit with that on the recrush screen. The three washing screens allowed all the fine material to be collected and flumed to the sand plant, which was based on a Hydrosizer unit that split material for subsequent precise grading. The concreting sand was pumped via a radially traversing gantry to a dewatering cyclone, thus producing a curved stockpile (Fig 44), while the building sand proceeded to a separate tower. The 4/20mm gravel, having been freed of lignite and thoroughly washed, was conveyed to the final screening and storage section. Here two double-deck screens separated the material into four single-size fractions, each of which was gravity-fed into one of the compartments of the 600-tonne total capacity storage hoppers. Beneath these was a blending system which allowed an accurately blended and weighed load to be discharged directly to vehicles via a lorry-loading conveyor. Each storage compartment was provided with an overflow conveyor to ground storage, and the blending conveyor was reversible to permit blended materials to discharge directly to stockpile (Fig 45).

An automated plant control centre provided full control and monitoring of the plant, and included crusher controllers, continuous-level monitoring and intelligent feed-rate control. The single operator was provided with a good view of the plant from an elevated position, as well as CCTV screens relaying from all key operations within the plant housings (see Fig 46). A modern delivery system was overseen by the weighbridge clerk. On arrival vehicles pulled up alongside an elevated intercom link and pneumatic conveying system, by which the clerk passed the driver a docket identifying the material required. By displaying this, drivers ensured that their vehicles were loaded with material of the correct specification, mainly from the lorry load-out system, or alternatively from ground stockpiles, after which they proceeded to the weighbridge to receive a conveyance ticket from the clerk. Between the weighbridge and the site exit was a compulsory automatic wheel washer which ensured minimum environmental impact as vehicles left the plant.

THREE

Impact

Sand and gravel landscapes

The landscapes associated with sand and gravel extraction are essentially transient. During the working lifetime of an individual quarry, extraction leads to the creation of large holes in the ground. Left alone, these will fill with water, in the case of those on the floodplain, or remain as excavated voids, in the case of pits worked above the water table. The degree of impact on the existing landscape is dependent on local geology and topography, water table level, and the method and rate of both extraction and restoration.

Industrial-scale sand and gravel quarrying has had a voracious appetite for the consumption of land. At the time of the Waters Report this was estimated to be, nationally, in the region of around 1200 acres (485 ha) per year. Since then, production levels have soared. To put this in the context of an individual site, over the course of its lifetime Hoveringham Quarry has worked at a rate of about 14 acres (c 5.5ha) a year, which amounts to a total of over 800 acres (324 ha) of land consumed in its 60 years of operation.

The working landscape

The nature of the impact of sand and gravel working on a specific area is dependent on its geology and method of working. To all intents and purposes, a dry working of a solid deposit such as the Sherwood Sandstone at Acton or Hilton looks to the layman much the same as traditional stone quarrying: a face gradually retreats in reaction to working which might include blasting or mechanical digging and shovelling. Traditional 'wet' working on the river terraces, on the other hand, presented a spectacle something more like fishing. In landscape terms, its main legacy was the strips of overburden which were cast back by dragline excavators into the worked-out pits (see Fig 25) which often remained in the form of a strangely corrugated water landscape (see Fig 69). Modern 'dry' terrace working, during which sites are mechanically dewatered, has more of the familiar appearance of major road construction. In the first phase of working, the removal of overburden, excavators and dumptrucks will be much in evidence, albeit hidden in the main behind screening bunds. During extraction proper, operations at ground level are often virtually invisible, as mobile plant excavates an ever larger hole. Often it is only from the air that it is apparent that mineral working is taking place at all.

Landscape case study: Shardlow Quarry

Quarrying operations on the current 200-hectare site adjacent to the Trent commenced in 1988, with the processing plant completed in 1991. The site produces up to 500,000 tonnes of material per year and current reserves are projected to sustain production until 2010. The deposit averages between 4m and 6m in depth and is overlain by 2m of soils and overburden which has been progressively stripped using hydraulic excavators and dumptrucks and stored for ongoing restoration work. Extraction is by 360° hydraulic excavator, which loads material into articulated dumptrucks for internal haulage to the plant. The site is liable to occasional flooding from the Trent, mainly in the winter months. During such periods extraction continues from a protected area built up during dry conditions, which holds about 100,000 tonnes of material. Figure 53 shows the site *c* 2003 in relation to the A50 trunk road and, towards the bottom, the site of the disused Castle Donington power station. The area bounded in red was worked in phases under permissions granted between 1981 and 2002. Extraction from the area bounded in yellow commenced in 2004. The processing plant is outlined in blue. The ground photographs (Figs 54 and 55) were taken in October 2005.

Figure 53 Shardlow Quarry from the air, *c* 2003, showing A50 trunk road and Shardlow village towards the top of picture and the decommissioned Castle Donington power station at the bottom (Reproduced by permission of Bluesky International Ltd)

Figure 54 Recently worked area at Shardlow Quarry, October 2005 (Photo: Tim Cooper/ ARCUS)

Figure 55 Worked-out area at Shardlow Quarry, October 2005. Note Weston Grange farm, the site of the operating company's noise tests, on the other side of the canal (Photo: Tim Cooper/ ARCUS)

In 1997 an access road was constructed to the new A50 so that vehicles serving the plant could avoid Shardlow village. At the same time the operating company, Hanson Aggregates, entered into an agreement with the Severn Trent Water company for the creation of storage reservoirs to allow water to be taken from the Trent. In this scheme, water taken from the river flows through a series of man-made lakes before being pumped to the nearby Church Wilne Treatment Works. The site is regulated by almost 30 planning conditions imposed by the County Council, European Union and Environment Agency which include water management, waste disposal and flood risk assessment. Environmental control measures incorporated at the site include vehicle wheel washing, bunded (ie environmentally screened) fuel tanks and a fully enclosed processing plant. Among the perimeter banks which have been built are some for acoustic screening; these incorporate trees and shrubs. The company conducts regular noise measurements next to the nearest noise-sensitive property, Weston Grange farm (Fig 55).

The original intention was for phased working with restoration to water for mixed conservation and recreation uses. However, more recent applications along these lines have faced objections from the nearby East Midlands Airport based on the increased risk of bird-strike likely to result from a proliferation of attractive wet landscapes. Restoration plans have been changed accordingly to landfill in the form of imported inert waste (ie construction rubble). European landfill regulations require that, due to the depth of the workings, all waste pit sides must be stable and lined with highly engineered impermeable clay. Regulations have also required the construction of an adjoining Waste Transfer Area so that all incoming loads can be checked and, if necessary, quarantined to avoid contamination of the site. Completed landfill areas will be returned to agriculture.

The worked-out landscape

While the working of sand and gravel deposits has an immediate impact on the landscape, the degree of permanence of this impact is dependent on the extent and method of site restoration. Until the early 1960s the tendency was for operators to leave their former workings 'to nature' which, in the case of the majority of pits in the Trent Valley, meant that they filled up with water. The main concern of gravel companies, of course, was to move on to the next productive site. Those who lived in, and used, the areas which had been worked often saw things differently, however. To take one example, the worked-out lagoons at Attenborough, interspersed with ridges and hummocks of abandoned spoil, were described by the Council for the Preservation of Rural England in 1962 as 'a scene of devastation that has to be seen to be believed' (*Nottingham Guardian Journal*, 4 April 1962) (Fig 56). The subsequent creation of Attenborough Nature Reserve (see below) was something of a watershed in attitudes, and the industry's perceived negative impact on the landscape is no longer subject to questions of whether, but rather of how, it is to be remedied.

The treatment of worked-out wet pits was one of the issues considered by the Waters Committee. Before the introduction of the Town and Country Planning Act, individual small pits were sometimes filled with domestic refuse, but an increasing number of environmental experiments were demonstrating that this could not be a viable large-scale solution. Whilst inert waste in the form of building rubble presented fewer ecological problems, the cost involved in transporting material to Trent Valley pits was deemed to be generally prohibitive. Another potential solution was the use of colliery waste and in the 1950s feasibility studies were carried out to ascertain economic viability. Despite small-scale applications, such as some filling of worked-out pits at Gunthorpe with waste from Gedling Colliery, the experiments concluded that the distance between the Nottinghamshire coalfield and the gravel quarries of the Trent Valley was generally too great for transport to be economical. Colliery waste was, however, the solution applied to Acton Quarry on the Sherwood Sandstone, when it was filled in the late 1980s after almost 200 years of continuous working (Fig 57).

Just when it looked like the problem was intractable, a solution appeared in the form of the newly opened Trent Valley power stations, which were looking to solve their own problem of the disposal of waste material from their boilers. Following positive feasibility studies, extensive use of pulverised fuel ash (PFA) for infilling of worked-out gravel pits commenced in 1950. Among the first power stations to take part in the scheme were Drakelow and Castle Donington. As increasing amounts of material became available the ultimate solution to a dual problem appeared to be in sight and soon lorries were taking ash from High Marnham to pits at Girton and Besthorpe, and from Staythorpe to Hoveringham and Gunthorpe. In cases where road transport was seen as either infeasible or undesirable, waste was pumped between sites by pipeline in the form of slurry. This was the solution implemented in the cases of pits at Stretton and Repton relative to the power station at Willington, and at Besthorpe, Girton and Meering in relation to the 'Marnham ash' provided by the power station on the

Figure 56 Worked-out gravel lagoons at Attenborough, *c* 1965: 'A scene of devastation that has to be seen to be believed' (By courtesy of Michael Arthur)

Figure 57 Acton Quarry – worked continuously for almost 200 years – finally being filled with colliery waste in 1989 (By courtesy of Bryan Atkin)

Figure 58 PFA being pumped into worked-out lagoons at Besthorpe/Meering Quarry, 1969 (By courtesy of QMJ Publishing Ltd)

other side of the river (Fig 58). Once this method was seen to be working it was more generally applied, leading, for example, to the replacement of the former vehicle traffic between Staythorpe and Hoveringham with a 10km pipeline. This delivered PFA to worked-out pits at Hoveringham at a rate of over 100,000 cubic metres per year until the closure of the power station in 1994.

However, by 1966 – the year that reclamation of lagoons at Inns & Co's pits at Besthorpe and Meering with Marnham ash was being acclaimed by government as a model of good practice – attitudes were changing. Plans to pump PFA from the new power station at Ratcliffe-on-Soar were abandoned due to a combination of pressure from Nottinghamshire Wildlife Trust (see below) and transport logistics. Growing concerns were also being raised with regard to the potentially negative impact of PFA itself on the environment. In any case, within 20 years of the material being hailed as the cure-all solution to gravel pit restoration, the more efficient second-generation Trent Valley power stations were no longer providing sufficient waste, and plans such as the filling of pits at Holme Pierrepont with material from Wilford were shelved. The problem had come full circle, and in the last decade of the 20th century the worked-out gravel pits of the Trent Valley were once again being allowed to remain as areas of water.

Landscape case study: the confluence of the Trent and Derwent

The once pastoral confluence of the Trent and Derwent has, in modern times, been transformed into one of the busiest rural landscapes in Britain. The village of Shardlow (Fig 59) is the starting point of the Trent and Mersey Canal, the great project of James Brindley and Josiah Wedgwood which, when completed in 1777, laid the foundation for much of the country's industrial development. Nowadays the main link between this area and the Potteries is provided by the A50 trunk road, visible here at its intersection with the M1 motorway. The edge of the town of Long Eaton at the top right corner of the photograph (taken c 2003) marks the southern limit of the Nottingham conurbation, while the southern limits of its Derby counterpart are just off the top of the photograph.

Otherwise this is, in settlement terms, a rural environment; the village of Shardlow is near the centre of the photograph and that of Castle Donington just encroaches at the bottom. Yet, in addition to the main lines of communication, the scene is dominated by industrial features, including four of the most productive gravel quarries in the Trent Valley and one of its first power stations. Just off the bottom of the picture is East Midlands Airport which, in recent years, has brought an international dimension to the area. To airborne visitors who care to look out of the window on landing, the sight that catches the eye is the characteristic light and dark landscape of sand and gravel country.

The history of large-scale gravel extraction in the area goes back to the surge in demand that coincided with the start of the Second World War. This saw Hilton Gravel Ltd open up pits at Hemington, Lockington and Shardlow and go on to dominate production in the area until the early 1960s. The second major impetus to the development of the area for aggregates was the building of the Midlands section of the M1 motorway from the mid-1950s. At the same time, the construction of Castle Donington power station further increased what was already a massive demand for concrete aggregates, and the expansion of extraction in the area was assured for much of the rest of the 20th century and beyond. The area in the centre of the photograph was worked extensively from the 1940s as 'Hemington Fields' and subsequently restored to agriculture using ash from Castle Donington.

From the air a clear distinction is visible between the light-coloured patches of current and recent extraction and the dark areas of former pits restored as lagoons. The supply of PFA from Castle Donington power station had dried up long before its decommissioning in 1994 and subsequent demolition, which has left local planners with something of a dilemma for this area. The 'natural' reclamation option for the low-lying gravel deposits is to water. This option was particularly favoured in the decade or so following the significant drought of 1976, when the local water authority supervised the excavation of pits to provide water storage as part of an integrated water supply scheme. In more recent years, however, there has been greater concern regarding the risk of flooding. Additionally, there is growing concern that the transfer of much former agricultural land to water has had a negative impact on the quality of the landscape and has created a new danger as a result of the number of birds attracted to the flight zone of the airport. For these reasons the planning process for extraction in this area has become particularly complex.

Figure 59
Confluence of Trent and Derwent from the air, c 2003; the site of the former Castle Donington power station is at bottom left (Reproduced by permission of Bluesky International Ltd)

The reclaimed landscape

If the main question facing the Waters Committee after the Second World War was maintaining supply of aggregates, planners in the ensuing years were almost equally preoccupied with problems of environmental dereliction. The new tone was set by the Town and Country Planning Act. Until then, only the most basic restoration of worked-out sites was expected. In 1947, the same year that the act came into force, an extension to Hoveringham Quarry was permitted by the local council on the main condition that 'before finally vacating the site, one month's notice [is] to be given to the Planning Authority and the whole site to be left clean and tidy and all plant, machinery and buildings removed unless otherwise agreed that certain buildings may remain' (see Appendix 4). Indeed, the Waters Committee had concluded that restoration should not be a condition of planning permissions and, in any case, preferred the term 'after-treatment' to 'restoration'.

However, growing environmental awareness provided the impetus for an emerging consent among planners that worked-out sites should be reclaimed at the earliest opportunity. In the Trent Valley, the abundance of PFA meant that in the period between the mid-1960s and early 1990s a great deal of land that had been quarried for gravel was able to be restored to dry ground level. To cite one example, up to 1993 some 54 hectares of former quarry in the vicinity of Hoveringham were restored using PFA, about 80% of which was given over to pasture, 18% to arable use and 4% to woodland. Although the use of PFA was not universally welcomed, it led to a markedly different restored landscape from, for example, the Thames Valley, in which the great majority of former workings were left to water.

The policy of converting former wet pits to amenity use that was actively pursued in the south-east of the country was also an option considered in the Trent Valley. During the 1960s worked-out areas at Attenborough, Hoveringham, Barton-under-Needwood, Branston, Swarkestone and Winthorpe were turned over for fishing and sailing. In 1966 Nottinghamshire County Council announced plans for the Trent Valley to be designated as a 'recreation centre', focused on the development of marina and watersports facilities at worked-out pits at Holme

Figure 60 National Watersports Centre, Holme Pierrepont, established on the site of former gravel workings and opened in 1973 (By courtesy of the National Watersports Centre)

Pierrepont and Colwick. By this time the industry was actively promoting the recreational use of former gravel pits and noted a shift in public opinion of gravel lagoons from eyesores to amenities. Not for the first time it was Hoveringham that took the lead, setting up its own Leisure Division to merge the company's aggregate and amenity interests in 1972. The following year Nottinghamshire County Council's vision came to fruition with the opening of the National Watersports Centre at Holme Pierrepont (Fig 60), which, like the earlier Colwick Water Park, was developed in co-operation with Hoveringham Gravels Ltd and the new Ministry for Sport.

In contrast to the limited conditions placed on Hoveringham Quarry in 1947, planning permission is now routinely linked to the submission of detailed restoration plans, meaning in effect that operating companies cannot work a new area until they have restored an earlier one. Current policy is informed by a growing number of national and supranational regulations governing restoration and landfill issues. A relatively limited supply of filling materials, in the form of either PFA or inert construction waste, makes restoring to dry land increasingly difficult. At the same time, however, there is a growing body of opinion which contends that the region has reached a point of 'water restoration overkill', leading to negative environmental impact, over-supply of amenity and an increasing danger of bird-strike to airborne traffic. The point has certainly been reached where restoration of former gravel workings is no longer a matter for operators and local councils alone, but for all parties interested in the long-term sustainability of the Trent Valley.

Landscape case study: the Trent downriver from Newark

This stretch of the River Trent, 14km (8.5 miles) as the crow flies, is one of the most extensively and continuously worked sand and gravel areas in the valley (Fig 61). Written in the landscape is the evidence of almost 70 years of endeavour, carried out by a number of the main operators in the industry's history and using a variety of methods of both extraction and restoration.

Moving downstream from Newark, the first area encountered is the Crankley Point pits (1) first opened up by Robert Teal Ltd in 1939–40 and then bought and subsequently enlarged by Hoveringham Gravels Ltd in the 1950s. At the peak of production, extraction was taking place on both sides of the river and material was taken from the northern area to the main plant for washing by a conveyor belt mounted on a bailey bridge. Despite being described as a 'problem pit' in the mid-1960s due to its negative impact on the landscape, further development was permitted until exhaustion in the mid-1970s. Since then the majority of pits have been restored to water amenity use, the main exception being a section to the west which was filled with PFA. A small complex of pools to the south of the site (1a) are those worked by the British Sugar factory, some of which were subsequently filled with its own processing waste. The Crankley Point site is discussed in greater detail below.

Adjacent to these pits to the north-east (2) is the Winthorpe (Holme) quarry, first worked by 'Lincoln and Hull' in 1939. With the exception of Crankley Point, this was the only pit granted permission by the authorities to be worked straight from the river through a cut in the bank, a practice that was subsequently prohibited. When first opened up, about 4 feet (1.5m) of topsoil and overburden were removed and used to build a flood bank between Winthorpe (railway) Crossing and the village of Holme to the north, a feature that has in recent years been incorporated into the Trent Valley Way long-distance footpath. When the decision was taken in the late 1940s to change the entrance to the pit so as to cause less damage to the bank, the initial breach was partly blocked by the sinking of a number of old boats. A large concrete barge currently visible at the landward side of Winthorpe Lake had been used as a provision store moored off Hull during the period of German bombing and was towed upriver following decommissioning in 1947.

No plant was ever built at Winthorpe because material was taken by barge to Hull for processing. The site was worked out by 1953 and the resulting lagoon was purchased by the River Trent Authority for amenity development. An area of similar size upriver in the vicinity of North Muskham (3) was again worked without plant, this time for material to be used in the improvement of the A1 during the 1950s and 60s. The complex of pits to the north at Cromwell (5) were also used for this scheme and the area has been worked again in recent years by the Lafarge company.

A deposit of gravel discovered in the 1930s at a bend in the river known to boatmen as Crow Tree (4a) is said, at 28 feet (10m), to be one of the deepest ever found. This was worked by 'Lincoln and Hull' using boat-mounted dredgers. Since 1990 the inland continuation of this deposit has been worked by the Tarmac company as their Langford Lowfields quarry (4). In keeping with modern practice the site is being restored progressively, in this instance as an ornithological reserve, which is referred to in greater detail below.

Another deep deposit of gravel, said to be over 25 feet (8m) thick, was worked by 'Lincoln and Hull' dredgers during the 1930s at an area known locally as Stones Close (6 and Fig 64), an operation that apparently led to occasional collapses of the bank and reprimands from the river authorities. According to former workers, the material here was of particularly high quality, with a low sand content: 'At Stones Close we took the gravel out right to the bank – it was lovely, it was the best gravel I've ever seen! It was all *peas and beans*[1] and gold in colour' (Jack Thornhill). The company subsequently worked the deposit inland, a process that has been continued in more recent years by Lafarge at their Besthorpe works (7).

The sand and gravel deposits in the vicinity of Besthorpe (8) have a long history of working by a succession of operators, including, in the 1950s alone, 'Lincoln and Hull', Star Gravels, Inns & Co and CAEC Howard of North Hykeham. Since the 1960s the main operators have been Inns & Co and its successors, Redland and Lafarge. The area was first opened up in 1939, like Winthorpe, by 'Lincoln and Hull' and was initially worked by slackline and mast (above, Chapter 2). As extraction progressed, a large area was opened up to the north (9) and the quarry subsequently became known as Besthorpe/Meering. Much of this site was restored to agriculture by Inns & Co in the 1960s, in a scheme that won praise at the time for being 'better organised at this quarry than any other in the Trent Valley'. Restoration was by means of PFA pumped across the river by pipeline from High Marnham power station.

In its heyday in the 1950s and 60s about two-thirds of the material won at Besthorpe was sent down river by barge to the Humber ports. The current operator, Lafarge, recommenced barge traffic from the quarry in 2000, this time to the new Europort near Wakefield. Present extraction takes place under a phased scheme, and large areas of the former workings have been turned into a nature reserve, discussed in detail below. The modern barge wharf at Besthorpe replaced that originally built by 'Lincoln and Hull' before the Second World War. On the opposite bank of the Trent, Carlton Wharf, believed to have been originally constructed by Robert Teal Ltd in the early years of the 20th century, is one of the genuine relics of the gravel industry.

Finally, Girton (10) was another quarry that had its origins in the successful prospecting by Frank and Durgin Thornhill on behalf of 'Lincoln and Hull' during the 1930s. Once commercial extraction was underway, the majority of material was sent by barge to Hull and Grimsby. Earlier workings were restored to agriculture using PFA from High Marnham power station and in recent years the site has been worked intermittently by the Tarmac company. The site is dealt with in greater detail below.

Figure 61 The Trent downriver from Newark, c 2003 (Reproduced by permission of Digital Globe)

Minerals planning and sustainable development

As the aggregates industry enters its second century its impact on the environment is regulated by a system of government policy statements and guidance aimed at informing decisions made by local planners within a conceptual framework of 'sustainable development'. In the context of minerals production this framework relates in the first instance to conservation of supplies, particularly through increased use of recycled materials, and minimisation of negative environmental impact. From the start of any new working, environmental management systems and impact assessments are put in place to cover issues such as soil management and the conservation of high-quality agricultural land. A number of issues regarding the impact of minerals working on communities are also dealt with, including opportunities for local consultation. Taking a wider view of community interest, mineral working is now severely restricted in areas of 'nationally designated landscape or archaeological value' and where there would be a negative impact on nature conservation or cultural heritage. Where mineral working does take place, sites are to be restored at the earliest possible opportunity to avoid the blight of dereliction that resulted from an earlier generation of working. Taken together, this means that minerals working is probably subject to a greater range of planning restrictions than any other industry. How these affect a single site can be seen by considering the recent planning conditions imposed on quarrying operations at Shardlow. When permission was granted for a new phase of working in 2003 conditions included:

- Advance planting of trees and shrubs to provide visual and acoustic screening and minimise wind-blown pollution; maintenance of planted areas; protection of parish boundary hedgerow; maintenance of hedgerows in general; provision of fences and gates
- Soil management: soil to be stripped in sequence and stored separately; creation of topsoil storage bunds to screen site; soil replacement; seeding
- Phased working and restoration plans to include details of existing ground levels; arrangements for importing inert landfill; location of haul roads
- Noise and dust monitoring schemes
- Flood risk assessment; water management (pumping); arrangements for silt disposal
- Protected species; in particular, habitats of badgers, water voles, bats and newts
- Archaeological watching brief

Complying with all planning conditions – and the above list is just a brief summary of what might be required – obviously entails operators in considerable expense and significantly affects decisions as to whether a potential working will be economically viable. A typical planning permission document will now run to around 20 pages. By way of comparison, Appendix 4 lists the nine conditions, contained in a single page, that regulated the first major extension to Hoveringham Quarry in 1947.

There is, of course, good reason why modern planning conditions are so numerous. As far back as the post-war Waters Report national and local government has had to face public criticism concerning the negative impact of aggregates working. In particular, Waters addressed the objection that alternative materials could be found that would obviate the need for large-scale workings in the Trent Valley, but concluded that:

> Competition between Trent Valley gravel and other aggregate and road making materials is of varied character but no alternative material threatens the predominance of valley gravel to an extent likely seriously to affect total output. Igneous rocks, quartzite and limestone are for some purposes preferred to gravel, and blast-furnace slag is extensively used in parts of the region for road work. The competition of these alternative materials has not, however, been such as to prevent an increase in the demand for gravel.
>
> (Waters Report, Part 3, p 22)

Since the 1950s an increasingly vocal environmental campaign forced a debate concerning the competing needs of the construction industry and the environment. A major milestone in this debate within the Trent Valley was the decision in the mid-1960s to turn redundant workings at Attenborough into a nature reserve (see below). By the early 1970s it had become apparent to local pressure groups that the best way forward was to work in partnership with planners and gravel companies to smooth the transfer of sites from extractive to amenity use. Within five years of opening, Attenborough had been designated as a Site of Special Scientific Interest (SSSI) and its delta area in particular was providing opportunities for the study of changes in biodiversity over time that were of international significance.

It was against this background that the Verney Report was commissioned, taking as one of its main subjects of enquiry the environmental impact of the industry and the potential for using greater amounts of recycled material. The report, published in 1976, has had a significant impact on attitudes since then, and over the past fifteen years the acknowledgement by aggregates companies of their responsibilities towards the natural environment has undergone a similar process of transformation to that observed in relation to archaeology (see below). As the beginning of a new millennium approached, the subject of a fiscal levy on aggregates production was raised seriously for the first time in almost four decades, this time with the explicit intention of improving operators' environmental performance. Despite concerted industry opposition in the form of a suggested alternative package of environmental initiatives, an Aggregates Levy of £1.60 per tonne was introduced in 2002. On behalf of the industry the Quarry Products Association (QPA) has continued to oppose what it calls the 'aggregates tax' on the grounds that it simply passes the cost burden onto the consumers of aggregates, almost half of which are in the public sector.

For a number of years the industry's representative body SAGA, and its successor the QPA, have been presenting awards to exemplary restoration schemes, and a perusal of the citations for each year demonstrates the real progress that has been made. The result of forty years of transformation of worked-out gravel pits into nature reserves is that few industries can genuinely claim to have been more actively involved in the causes of environmental sustainability, biodiversity and, following more recent government directives, geodiversity.[2] A number of the historically significant (or notorious, depending on one's view) gravel-working areas of the Trent Valley now count among the most important habitat creation schemes in the country. A survey of just a few of them highlights their significance.

Conservation case studies

Attenborough Nature Reserve

Sand and gravel quarrying in the vicinity of Attenborough commenced in the late 1920s on land between the main railway line and the Trent (see above, Chapter 1). The first phase of extraction, initially using a dredging pump, worked gradually northwards and was completed in 1939. Since then, extraction has been by mechanical excavators and progressed southwards, with material being transported back to the processing plant by barge. In recent years extraction has crossed the county boundary (the River Erewash) and currently takes place near Long Eaton in Derbyshire. By the time current reserves are worked out, the quarry will have been in continuous production for almost a century, a remarkable achievement in an industry generally regarded as transient.

Figure 63 Sir David Attenborough at the opening of the new visitor centre, Attenborough Nature Reserve, 2005 (By courtesy of Nottinghamshire Wildlife Trust)

Figure 62 Attenborough Quarry and Nature Reserve from the air, *c* 2003, with the area of the Nature Reserve shaded and showing (1) site of processing plant, (2) Attenborough historic village, (3) site of visitor centre and (4) current excavation. The dotted line represents the channel used by barge traffic. The River Erewash joins the Trent from the top left of the photograph (Reproduced by permission of Bluesky International Ltd)

However, during that time the site has not been without its problems. The fact that, for the past 30 years, extraction has taken place in Derbyshire and processing in Nottinghamshire has meant that the planning process has been particularly complex. In addition, successive operators of the site have been subject to the complaint that, to quote a recent planning review, 'the plant site is poorly located, being in a residential area where it causes noise and dust pollution.' Not without justification, successive owners of the site have pointed out that it could equally be argued that the residential area is 'poorly located', arriving as it did when sand and gravel extraction was well underway. In the mid-1960s, up to which point former workings were simply abandoned, forming lagoons, the quarry attracted vociferous criticism from, among others, the Campaign for the Protection of Rural England (see above).

Using the momentum generated by this criticism the Nottinghamshire Wildlife Trust promoted a campaign to use the area for nature conservation. The resulting Attenborough Nature Reserve was formally opened by the naturalist and broadcaster David Attenborough on 30 April 1966 (Fig 62). In more than 40 years' existence the site has been a model of successful co-operation between conservation bodies and minerals operators. The present site comprises 100ha of former gravel pits and 145ha of marginal vegetation, offering a variety of habitats on the course of an important bird migration route. The Reserve is owned by the present gravel operators, Cemex, and jointly managed with the Nottinghamshire Wildlife Trust with support from the local council. SSSI status reflects the success with which diverse habitats have been created, including wet meadow and marsh, and a 'delta' originally laid down by silt streams from the gravel workings. This area, to which public access is prohibited, has been allowed to develop 'naturally' and as such provides a valuable source of long-term ecological data.

Since its inception, the Reserve has made an incomparable contribution to biodiversity values within the Trent Valley and thus to one of the key aims of the UN convention of 1992. To take birds and wildfowl alone, 89 species have been recorded on a single day in the main spring migration period and at any time of year visitors are likely to see over 50 species. The popularity of the Reserve with the public led to the opening of a new visitor centre by Sir David Attenborough in 2005 (Fig 63). The building, commissioned to a 'visionary eco-design', includes education facilities, meeting rooms, interactive displays, nature shop and café, and was brought to realisation through co-operation between local and national conservation and funding bodies and the quarry operators. In 2006 the operator of Attenborough Quarry, Cemex, was awarded the Cooper Heyman Trophy for its part in the development of the reserve, hailed by the Quarry Products Association as 'a credit to this industry'.

Besthorpe Nature Reserve

Gravel working has taken place in the vicinity of Besthorpe almost continuously since the first pit was opened by 'Lincoln and Hull' in 1939. The French company Lafarge is currently working an adjacent area of over 330ha, which is projected to be productive until 2014. Since 2000 the building of a new riverside wharf, with the aid of a Department of Transport freight grant, has enabled material once again to be transported by barge, nowadays to the new Europort near Wakefield.

The earliest workings have been mainly restored to agriculture since the 1960s using PFA pumped across the Trent via a pipeline from High Marnham power station. More recent workings have been restored to water in the form of two separate conservation areas. Besthorpe North, to the north of Trent Lane, includes an area of managed reed beds, orchid areas, and maintained open shingle and gravel areas aimed at providing habitat for a number of bird species, including little ringed plover. Besthorpe South includes two water meadows designated an SSSI in 1988, which contain a distinctive and nationally rare plant community which includes species such as Yorkshire fog, great burnet, lady's bedstraw, common knapweed, meadow vetchling, and pepper saxifrage.

A management regime applied to the meadows includes the cutting of hay in late summer followed by the introduction of sheep to carry out 'aftermath grazing'. An old borrow pit fringed by willows contains a varied aquatic flora including spiked water milfoil and common water crowfoot. The willow is cut on a rotational basis to ensure that light can reach the water in order to enhance the aquatic habitat. To the south of the meadows a former gravel pit now known as Mons Pool provides habitat for a colony of nesting cormorants and a heronry, as well as a wide variety of winter visitors, including tufted duck, pochard, and goosander. Both areas are managed by Nottinghamshire Wildlife Trust on a lease from the gravel operator and are open to the public. There are two bird-watching hides with boardwalks providing wheelchair access. Recent workings are also being converted to wildlife habitats in the form of lakes with islands (Fig 64).

Langford Lowfields

Extraction of gravel from Langford Lowfields started in 1990, and based on current annual production of 400,000 tonnes, has reserves estimated to last until 2017. In keeping with modern planning regulations the quarry is being restored in phases, in this instance as a major wildfowl reserve. About a quarter of the site has already been restored and is managed by the Royal Society for the Protection of Birds (RSPB), which will assume control of the whole site once extraction has ended. Tom Dodsley, who in 2005 was area manager for the operating company, Tarmac, viewed the site as a good example of modern phased restoration:

Figure 64 View north towards the Trent near Collingham, April 2006. In the centre is the current Besthorpe Quarry being worked, with phased restoration, by the Lafarge company. A barge, fed by conveyor from the plant, can be seen in the big loop in the river to the left of the photograph. Visible towards the top is Besthorpe Nature Reserve's 'Mons Pool' area, itself a former gravel working, with its heronry in the middle. Worked-out areas to the immediate south of the gravel plant, in the centre of the photograph, can be seen in the process of landscaping for restoration with water and islands. The area by the river to the bottom left of the photograph, known locally as 'Stones Close', was one of the first areas in the Trent Valley to be worked commercially for gravel; together with the area in the loop of the river to the immediate north, it has since been restored to agriculture (By courtesy of Lafarge Aggregates Ltd)

We try to come up with mixed restoration schemes as we now realise the potential problems of all-water schemes. You look back at some of the landfill restorations of a few years ago and they were not entirely satisfactory. We are restoring Langford so that it can provide a migrating habitat for the bittern. It's being restored progressively, in close co-operation with the RSPB who have planted some 70,000 reeds, and it looks very good. We spent about £200,000 this summer [2005] doing restoration work there. I go round the sites regularly and check that the restoration schemes are up to date; it's in our interest to restore as soon after excavation as possible.

The creation of some 40ha of reed beds will double the total amount of this habitat within Nottinghamshire and make a significant contribution towards the national target of creating 1200ha of new reed beds by 2010. As well as helping to meet both regional and national biodiversity targets, it is specifically intended that the site will support two or three breeding pairs of bittern, a species currently on the endangered list. In common with most sites in the Trent Valley region the nature reserve will be well placed to service both north–south and east–west bird migration routes. The site also has a high potential for amenity use and will include a visitor centre and footpaths.

Hilton Gravel Pits

The first pits were dug in the Sherwood Sandstone at Hilton at the end of the 19th century and the site was subsequently developed by the local landowning family, the Spurriers (see above, Chapter 1). Hilton Gravel went on to become one of the most successful Trent Valley gravel companies, being eventually taken over by Blue Circle Aggregates in 1967. By the end of the 1970s the majority of the workings at Hilton were exhausted and, despite the prevailing wisdom of refilling dry pits with household refuse, these were 'left to nature' with very little landscaping taking place apart from some tree planting.

The area now has SSSI status and comprises a reserve of 29ha with open water, marsh, carr, and woodland habitats which is managed by the Derbyshire Wildlife Trust. The reserve successfully supports a number of nationally endangered species, including the great crested newt and black poplar. Fifteen species of dragonflies and damselflies have been recorded, the old silt settling beds providing a good sheltered feeding area which has also encouraged the establishment of plant species such as southern marsh orchids and common twayblade. The ponds and lakes attract varied waterfowl species, including coot, great crested grebe, and tufted duck, and there has been a rare British sighting of the Slavonian grebe. Public access is facilitated by a network of footpaths, some of which are boarded for ease of wheelchair access.

Aggregates and archaeology

Perhaps no other region of the country has brought the potentially competitive relationship between minerals extraction and archaeology into such sharp focus as the Trent Valley. The period in which the aggregates industry developed in the region has coincided with a growing appreciation of the rich archaeological resource of the floodplain and river terraces of the Trent. Indeed, current knowledge of human activity in Britain during the Palaeolithic period (c 500,000 to 35,000 years ago) is almost exclusively derived from evidence uncovered during sand and gravel extraction. The often difficult relationship between aggregates and archaeology is based on the central irony that the recovery of evidence of the past is heavily dependent on the industry which has the potential for destroying it. The negative impact of quarrying in all forms was highlighted by the 'Monuments at Risk Survey' commissioned by English Heritage in 1995. This found that, between 1945 and 1995, 12% of the loss of, or damage to, archaeological sites in England could be said to have occurred as a consequence of mineral extraction. Against this, there has been a long history of co-operation between aggregates companies and archaeologists in the Trent Valley, even before the introduction of recent legislation. Since then, an enormous quantity of archaeological investigation in the region has been funded by aggregates companies. The introduction of the Aggregates Levy Sustainability Fund (ALSF) in 2002, by directing funding specifically at research, has further increased the industry's contribution to our understanding of the past. At the beginning of the 21st century it is clear that the interests of archaeology, heritage and aggregates are inextricably linked.

The antiquarian tradition and isolated finds

The importance of river gravels for preserving evidence of the human and environmental past was recognised at an early stage of antiquarian and archaeological enquiry, and by the late 19th century investigators were specifically targeting gravel pits in the Trent Valley. As well as helping to illuminate the prehistory of the region, these early pioneers often provided incidental descriptions of the quarries themselves and the methods by which they were being worked. First among the more prominent figures was Fred Davey, a telegraph operator for the Midland Railway, whose amateur antiquarian interest was mainly in Palaeolithic flake tools. Roaming the often haphazard gravel workings of the Beeston area of Nottingham at the turn of the 20th century, he taught the workmen how to recognise stone tools and, at the cost of a few pence slipped into pockets, built up a substantial collection.

Next came A L Armstrong, a familiar figure at gravel quarries at Hilton and Willington in the first quarter of the 20th century, who went on to amass the largest single collection of stone artefacts from the Trent Valley. The path beaten by Armstrong was followed in the mid-century by G F Turton, whose researches, mainly conducted in the same quarries, provided the material for much of the analysis of the prehistory of the region published from the 1960s onwards. Armstrong's notebooks, in particular, are full of incidental references to gravel working which contribute to our understanding of the early history of the industry (Fig 65). An extract from the late 1930s provides a flavour of the material:

Hilton, April 1/39. W.H. [W. Hanbury, a geologist] and self. Spent about 6½ hours in the pit on west side of the road, with gratifying results. Gravel is being worked by mechanical excavator and the face is rapidly being pushed back. A fine section was exposed and the contorted beds observed on the first visit were again conspicuous … At the N.W. corner of the pit, where work was in progress, I took out a magnificent middle Acheulian bi-face [hand axe] of perfect type, 1' 6" above the base mark and lying nearly horizontal. Had to wade to get it, but its quality was worth a wetting![3]

It was not long before both the gravel operators and individual workers realised that the remains of the past were an interesting by-product of their labour. By the early 1950s, as the scale of gravel working increased, so did the number of finds, some of which went to the museums of the region while others remained in private hands. Deg Bellamy claims to have come across at least ten mammoth's teeth during his time at Girton and Besthorpe quarries, and so common were such finds by then that 'the museums had got them and no-one wanted them'. In consequence, together with various pieces of mammoth tusk, one fine example of his discoveries of mammoth molars now forms an attractive feature of his garden.

Increasingly, the archaeological and fossil remains emerging from the gravel pits of the region became the stock-in trade of the local press. In 1954 the

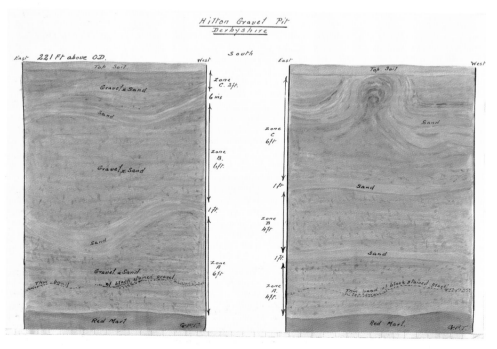

Figure 65 Section drawing of gravel deposits at Hilton Quarry, c 1950, by George Turton (By courtesy of Derby Museum and Art Gallery)

Figure 66 Isolated finds on display at Attenborough Quarry, *c* 1965 (By courtesy of Cemex UK)

Newark Advertiser eagerly reported finds, including the 'tooth of a prehistoric brontosaurus' and an 'earthenware pot of Roman Coins', that had been unearthed at Hoveringham Quarry in recent years, and former workers remember the excitement that was generated on such occasions. Hoveringham and Girton were sites where mammoth fossils were periodically discovered, along with fossilised trees, or 'bog oaks' as they were known in the gravel business. Terry Cliff remembers the occasion of such a find at Hilton Gravels' Clay Mills Quarry near Burton upon Trent: 'They hit some 'bog oak' which was dug out very carefully, dried slowly over a number of years and then made into the boardroom table of Hilton Gravel. It took six people to move it.'

Trent Gravels was one of the companies which recognised quite early on the value, both in the interests of archaeology and public relations, of keeping finds together on site. By the early 1960s quite a collection was on display in a cabinet in the company's offices in Attenborough, including mammoth's teeth, Bronze Age artefacts and Roman pottery (Fig 66). However, to the academic establishment it was becoming increasingly apparent that in order to protect both individual discoveries and, even more importantly, to record the archaeological context in which they were found, a clear government policy would be required.

Towards a policy for aggregates and archaeology

The Council for British Archaeology (CBA) was of the opinion as early as 1946 that archaeology and the aggregates industry were heading on a collision course. Its submission to the Waters Committee headed 'Urgent archaeological problems associated with modern methods of gravel working' is, again, equally of interest for its observations concerning contemporary quarrying methods:

> The losses to our knowledge of Palaeolithic man have been most grievous during recent years, and the least we may hope for is that some typical sections of gravel of archaeological interest may be preserved for future researches ... All workings used to be dug by hand and gravel-pits were numerous and generally small. Today the extraction of gravel is almost entirely done by great mechanical grabs, and the diggings are fewer but more extensive. Even the removal of the topsoil by hand has been superseded by the employment of improved but, from our standpoint, all-devastating plant. The manual work produces a vertical section, reveals every bed from grass to bench and seldom seriously injures contained antiquities and bones. The modern method gives a sloping face and furrowed bench, always obliterates the strata, usually shatters relics and destroys most animal remains.

> Countless hand-axes have been recovered by the manual labourers, generally when passing gravel through graded screens. But the latest machines include apparatus for washing and separating the materials taken up by the grabs and breaking the gravel into different sizes. Since they can deal with tons of material in a few minutes, it is difficult for the workman to pick out antiquities even if he can recognise them ... Against the old methods of extracting gravel it may be advanced that it has enriched only the cabinets of collectors, not all of whom can be called scientists, and that it has profited the labourer in transactions of undoubted illegality. Its merits outweigh these considerations for it has afforded wonderful scope to the student; it has been the means of proving the geological antiquity of man; and it has caused innumerable relics to be preserved. Little can be said in favour of the modern methods. Besides their capability for destroying so much, they have been responsible for the extinction of a type of workman who, if properly instructed and made to take an interest in the relics of antiquity, could be a valuable helper.

> (National Archives HLG 89/84)

Following the publication of the Waters Report, the Ministry of Works spent much of the 1950s in discussion with its colleagues at the Ministry for Housing and Local Government in an attempt to formulate a planning policy that addressed fears such as those expressed by the CBA while accommodating the large-scale allocations of gravel-producing land that had been made to the industry. The first of a number of attempted compromises appeared in 1959:

When such land contains scheduled or unscheduled monuments [the Ancient Monuments Board] may wish to object to the proposal, or agree only on certain conditions (e.g. that facilities are given for archaeological excavation prior to working). It has therefore been agreed with [the Dept of Works] that, when we propose to object to intended new sand and gravel working, or to acquiesce only on conditions, we shall consult them ...

(National Archives WORK 14/2980)

The determining factor as to whether a proposed gravel working contained a monument, scheduled or otherwise, was whether it was marked on the six-inch edition of the Ordnance Survey. However, a nationwide study by the Royal Commission on Historical Monuments (RCHM) published in 1960 as 'A Matter of Time' concluded that 'there are many important monuments which lie on sand and gravel sites which are as yet unscheduled'. In the light of this lack of clear definition the CBA's Field Monument Committee's report of 1969 called for 'sympathetic treatment of unscheduled sites lacking statutory protection [which is] particularly important on the riverine sand and gravel terraces where there tend to be heavy concentrations of sites which are vulnerable to rapid extraction.' The report went on to recommend an expansion of the number of scheduled monuments within England, the commissioning of systematic aerial photographic surveys, local recording of sites considered to be at risk, and state guardianship of deserted settlement sites in particular (National Archives WORK 14/2980). Throughout the 1970s and 1980s, despite the comparatively forward-thinking policies adopted by some companies, most of the archaeological intervention on aggregates sites was conducted on a 'rescue' basis. At the same time, however, an increasing number of quarrying operations were taking place in accordance with a code of practice drawn up in partnership with the Confederation of British Industry (CBI), which sought 'to promote co-operative and effective working relationships between mineral operators, planners and archaeologists'.

A significant change to the prevailing planning climate followed the issue, in 1990, of the Department of the Environment's Planning Policy Guidance notes 15 and 16, which acted as supplements to the Ancient Monuments and Archaeological Areas Act of 1979 and the Town and Country Planning Act as revised in 1990. For the first time, developers and minerals operators were under an obligation to fund any archaeological investigation deemed necessary on the affected site. In addition, the guidance gave further protection to Scheduled Monuments by prohibiting mineral extraction in such areas in all but exceptional circumstances. While the impracticability of preserving all archaeological remains was recognised, provision was made for their assessment relative to regional and national importance. Where preservation *in situ* was deemed to be impractical, sites should be surveyed, excavated or otherwise appropriately recorded following an initial process of evaluation. The planning policy guidance now in place, together with the ALSF, means that aggregates companies now have a major stake in the investigation and preservation of the archaeological record of the Trent Valley.

Aggregates, archaeology and the Trent Valley

The public relations potential of archaeological and palaeontological discoveries was first recognised by the industry in the early 1950s. So far as the Trent Valley region was concerned, it was Hoveringham Gravels that first took advantage. At its main quarry the first mammoth's tooth had been discovered in the mid-1950s and following some significant finds of tusks, the company decided to adopt the mammoth as its brand mark (see Fig 21). In the summer of 1961 Hoveringham held what was probably the earliest public relations event at a British gravel quarry when it invited the public to witness a 'mammoth hunt' which was to take place in one of its worked-out pits. Having found a number of significant remains over a period of a few years, company officials had become convinced that the entire skeleton of a mammoth must be lurking in the mud of the pool in which the original remains were located. The event generated a good deal of publicity and helped to detract attention from the fact that the pit – in which 'frogmen' from Mansfield Police, the Sub-Aqua Clubs of Nottingham and Sheffield, and the Mansfield Underwater Swimming Club foraged in vain for almost ten hours – was about to be pumped full of waste ash from Staythorpe power station. According to an article in the trade press, the mammoth hunt started with high hopes but

> the graph of optimism took a really sharp nose dive when it was learned that a huge mound of spoiled earth on the bank of the lake had been bulldozed back into the pit since the tusk had been found. But optimism is apparently a characteristic of frogmen – and of Hoveringham Gravels Ltd – for the search is continuing.
>
> (*Cement Lime and Gravel*, June 1961, p 190)

In the Trent Valley, professional archaeologists, representatives of local planning and education authorities, museums, and archaeological societies came together under the auspices of the CBA in the form of the Trent Valley Archaeological Research Committee, formed in 1967. Among donations received were significant contributions from the Hilton, Hoveringham, and Trent Gravels companies. The general spirit of co-operation has been recognised more recently with the formation of the Trent Valley GeoArchaeology group (TVGA) in 2001, comprising archaeologists, geologists, heritage and conservation experts, and industry representatives, a body created to promote research into the sustainable use of the valley. Under its auspices the first major synthesis of archaeological research in the region was published in 2004 under the title *Trent Valley Landscapes*. This demonstrated that research based at gravel quarries up and down the valley had helped enormously to confirm the national, and arguably international, importance of the region in understanding both environmental development and the human past. In 2006 the group oversaw the publication of a booklet entitled *Making Archaeology Matter: Quarrying and Archaeology in the Trent Valley*, aimed at providing an accessible introduction to the key issues.

Some of the key sand and gravel sites in the Trent Valley, and the finds associated with them, are summarised in Table 1. The research at Trent Valley gravel sites has helped recover not just individual finds but significant elements

Table 1

Quarry site	Principal discoveries
Alrewas (Whitemoor Haye)	Woolly rhinoceros
Attenborough	Mammoth teeth Bronze Age metalwork Roman pottery
Carlton	Bronze Age metalwork
Colwick	Ancient oak trunks Bronze Age metalwork Anglo-Saxon fish weir
Elvaston	Bronze Age metalwork
Girton	Bronze Age burnt mounds Late Bronze Age pottery concentration
Gonalston	Iron Age roundhouse
Hemington	Medieval bridge foundations Medieval fish weir Medieval mill dam
Hilton	Palaeolithic hand axes
Holme Pierrepont	Ancient tree trunks Bronze Age metalwork Bronze Age log boats Iron Age/Roman domestic enclosures
Hoveringham	Mammoth tusks, teeth Bronze Age barrow cemetery
Langford Lowfields	Ancient tree trunks Neolithic/Bronze Age human remains Bronze Age metalwork
Lockington	Bronze Age metalwork
North Hykeham	Palaeolithic hand axes
Norton Disney	Palaeolithic hand axes
Shardlow	Bronze Age log boats Bronze Age metalwork
Staythorpe (power station)	Mesolithic human remains
Whisby	Mammoth tusk Palaeolithic hand axes
Willington	Palaeolithic hand axes Bronze Age burnt mound

of the prehistoric and historic landscape. One such site, a complex of field systems and settlement remains in the vicinity of the village of South Muskham, has been designated as an area of special archaeological interest within which aggregates working will not be permitted for the foreseeable future. Among the sites highlighted above are a number that are of either national or international importance; these are discussed further below.

Alrewas (Whitemoor Haye)

The remains of four woolly rhinoceros were discovered in 2002. Both the site and the best-preserved remains are of international importance.

Girton

In 1998 a remarkable concentration of almost 600 plain and decorated pottery sherds dating to the late Bronze Age or early Iron Age, many in fresh condition, were located within a thin layer of dark sand incorporating charcoal, fragments of burnt bone, and numerous heat-shattered pebbles. One side of the deposit had been truncated by machining and it may have originally extended over a roughly circular area at least 7m in diameter.

Holme Pierrepont

Since the 1950s a number of finds of log boats have been made here, including three examples in a single site.

Langford Lowfields

An exceptional find of human and animal remains, which, it has been suggested, accumulated at a log-jam in a former channel of the Trent, was recovered at the quarry in 1996. The site is unparalleled in the Trent Valley and two possible explanations for the deposit have been put forward. The first is that major flooding caused people and animals to be swept downstream until becoming entangled in a blockage of tree trunks and brushwood. The alternative theory is that the deposit is associated with riverside mortuary rituals, suggestions of which have been discovered at other sites.

Shardlow

A spectacular find in 2001 comprised a largely intact log boat jammed against a number of oak logs and containing several blocks of Bromsgrove sandstone, the nearest source of which would have been some 3km upstream (Fig 67). Since then another well-preserved log boat has been found at the quarry and is being preserved *in situ*. Together these finds provide important evidence of riverine activity in the Bronze Age.

Figure 67 The Shardlow log boat, with its cargo of sandstone blocks (Photo: Jon Humble)

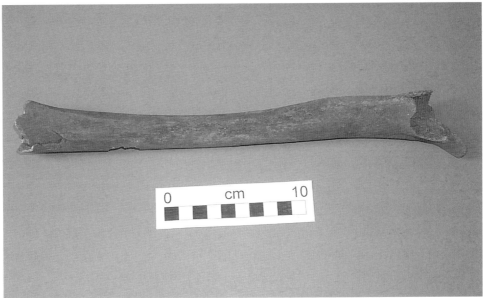

Figure 68 Human female femur from Staythorpe (Photo: ARCUS)

Staythorpe Borrow Pits

Mesolithic human remains were recovered from former river channels here in 2001 (Fig 68), along with animal remains showing evidence of butchery. As well as furthering our knowledge of human use of animal and plant resources in this period the site has emphasised the potentially vital role of analysis of ancient river channels ('palaeochannels') in understanding prehistory.

The historic environment

In 1965 a meeting of local residents was told that a proposed extension of gravel working in their area threatened to 'wipe away the village of Hoveringham' (*Nottingham Guardian Journal*, 29 February 1965). From around this time there have been continuing concerns regarding the isolation of the historic core of Attenborough village amid a chain of worked-out gravel lagoons. Understandable reactions such as these arise from concepts of community, identity, and history which, when merged, might be defined as the 'historic environment'. But how do we make value judgements with regard to such an abstract concept? Is a medieval castle more worthy of preservation than a 19th-century cotton mill? Should more effort be expended on saving the integrity of a medieval village core than a 20th-century new town? One specific example might suffice to highlight the complexity of what might at first sight appear straightforward questions. Less than a generation ago the relics of the lead mining industry in the Derbyshire Peak District were regarded as a blemish on the landscape, and farmers who ploughed them out, usually on the grounds of their potential danger to livestock, were applauded as 'improvers'. Today their successors are more likely to face prosecution for the wilful destruction of a historic monument. How, then, do we evaluate the significance within the 'historic environment' of a similarly transient extractive industry like gravel quarrying – now and in the future?

The most useful analytical tool that has emerged in recent years to help with qualitative judgements regarding landscape elements is 'Historic Landscape Characterisation' (HLC), although the concept still awaits a sufficiently precise definition. The best definition in the present context is probably that used by Nottinghamshire County Council Planning Department in its latest evaluation of minerals resources in the region. This suggests that Historic Landscape Character 'gives expression to the varying degrees of historical depth visible in today's landscapes'; in other words, it tries to resolve the debate expressed in simple terms above. The most significant challenge so far to emerge from the concept of HLC is the English Heritage discussion document *Change and Creation: Historic Landscape Character 1950–2000* (2004). This is an attempt to bring landscapes created, developed or affected by historical processes in the recent past into the discussion of historic environment and 'heritage'. Among the questions it raises are: 'What does the material legacy of the second half of the twentieth century mean to us as people who lived in it?' and 'When should we start to value it as part of the historic environment, as part of our common heritage?' The document concludes with a bold statement: 'It seems wrong to view the later twentieth century merely as a pollutant, something that has devalued and destroyed what went before. The process of landscape change – its time-depth, or 'stratigraphy' – is recognised and celebrated for earlier periods. The twentieth century should be no different.'

It is arguable that no other industry has had a greater influence on the creation of the world we inhabit – that which emerged in the second half of the 20th century – than sand and gravel extraction. How do we start transforming our view of the industry from one of polluter and destroyer to a 'celebrated' part of our heritage?

Landscape case study: South Muskham and Crankley Point

The modification of the landscape by human action is perhaps more strikingly evident here than at any other stretch of the Middle Trent Valley. A number of features are detectable in the aerial photograph taken in 1971 which demonstrate how modern gravel working has been incorporated into the historic landscape (Fig 69). The channel of the Trent which bisects the photograph was subject to improvement in the 16th century by the Sutton family in order to power their mills at Kelham House. At this time, the main Newark channel, to the right of the photograph, fell out of use to traffic. Earlier arrangements were restored in 1772 when the recently formed Trent Navigation Company carried out improvements to the Newark channel. The two watercourses converge at the outer limit of Newark, forming a spit of land known as Crankley Point, visible to the right of the photograph. From the air, however, the most prominent features are two straight lines: the course of the old Great North Road leaving Newark (bisected in turn by a long-distance drainage ditch originating in a spring in the nearby Kelham Hills) and the course of the East Coast mainline railway.

On the ground, the remains are visible of five earthwork features dating to the Civil War period, in which the town of Newark saw significant action. In the spring of 1644 a 7000-strong Parliamentarian army with thirteen siege guns crossed the Trent at Muskham Bridge (visible towards the centre of the photograph) and gained control of the land known as 'The Island' between the two branches of the river. The result of the consequent intensive military activity in the area is an unparalleled concentration of landscape features, primarily in the form of defensive earthworks and artillery platforms.

Industrial gravel-working at Crankley Point (1, 2) was first undertaken in the late 1930s by Robert Teal Ltd of Carlton-on-Trent, one of only two operators given licence to work straight from a cut in the river bank, the other being 'Lincoln and Hull' at its adjacent Winthorpe pit, opened in 1939. Both pits were developed rapidly to meet the huge demand for concrete for war defences and runways. The Crankley Point quarry was purchased from Teal's, and subsequently extended (3, 4), by Hoveringham Gravels Ltd in the early 1950s. By the mid-1960s the company had begun removing gravel from its reserve land to the west (5), so that the combined workings now straddled the Great North Road. Much of the gravel from this area was used for the Newark bypass and improvements to the A1 to the north of the town. Described by the Trent Valley Gravel Review as a 'problem pit', rapid excavation of allocated reserves had left behind 'a trail of unsightly dereliction'. The parallel strips of land left within the lagoons after working, visible in the photograph (3, 5), were formed by the 'casting back' of overburden into the wet pit (see above, Chapter 2).

South
Muskham

Mainline railway

⑧

⑦

⑤ ✦

③

① ✦

Great North Road

④

② ✦

✦

✦

✦

⑥

✦ Civil War Earthworks

6 197

7145

Figure 69 South
Muskham and
Crankley Point in
1971 (Reproduced b
permission of Blom
Aerofilms Ltd)

In 1965 permission was granted for the British Sugar Corporation to extract gravel from about 6ha of land in the immediate vicinity of its factory and adjacent to the Hoveringham works, and to use the resulting pits for the dumping of processing waste (6). By 1966 Hoveringham had started to work its reserves to the immediate north of the Trent (7), using a conveyor mounted on a bailey bridge to transport material to the plant. Crankley Point was thus the first major gravel excavation to take place on both sides of the river. At this time the company was pursuing the possibility of extending its working northwards, a move resisted by the Ministry of Housing and Local Government which was 'loathe to see the village of South Muskham engulfed' and which preferred a south-easterly extension of working 'if this was absolutely necessary', or even north-eastwards, beyond the railway (8). In the event, the company took the latter option and all remaining reserves were worked out by the mid-1970s.

Comparison of Fig 69 with a recent map (*c* 2000, Fig 70) shows the cumulative effects on the landscape of both gravel working and after-treatment. Most noticeable are the extensive tracts of water formed by the second and third main phases of working. The lake (1) to the immediate south of the village of South Muskham is currently in use by a sailing club and the complex of six lakes to the east (2) – now known as the 'A1 Gravel Pits' – is a favourite location for coarse fishing. This pastime is also popular at lakes formed when the original plant area was worked for gravel at the end of the permission period (3, 4). The earlier pit (5) to the immediate south of the river, complete with its original overburden strips and subsequent planting of trees, has been transformed into habitat for a variety of bird species, and is rated as having significant ornithological value. The expanse of water with overburden strips (6) to the west of the Great North Road has subsequently been returned to agricultural use following infilling with PFA from the former Staythorpe power station. Further gravel working that took place in the vicinity of the sugar factory has been left in the form of lagoons (7). On the ground, remains of the former extensive gravel working is all but invisible and it is the sugar factory which now dominates an otherwise apparently rural area on the outskirts of Newark.

A large area around the village of South Muskham (yellow shading), has in recent years been designated as an 'Area of Archaeological Importance' following consultation between archaeologists, local planners and central government. Fieldwalking programmes in the area, as well as the gradual accumulation of isolated finds, have shown that the parish contains one of the densest areas of known archaeological remains in the Trent Valley. As an area of major local and regional importance within which a good deal of further study needs to be undertaken, it is out of bounds for gravel extraction for the foreseeable future.

Towards an industrial archaeology of the sand and gravel industry

Any understanding of the true significance of the sand and gravel industry must include an analysis of its physical impact on, and integration within, the landscape. It must also consider the spatial relationships between the different stages of production, including extraction, processing, and transport, as well as between the various elements of the production process itself. These might include processing plant, storage areas, weighbridges, wharves, offices, workshops, ancillary buildings, water management features, and internal haulage tracks. The difficulty that is immediately faced, however, is one that, historically at least, has not applied equally to all forms of mineral extraction. Stone quarry landscapes, for example, can sometimes remain available for interpretation for a considerable time. As we have seen, it is now a requirement of gravel workings that they should be reclaimed as soon as possible. Current policy is expressed succinctly in Minerals Planning Guidance 7: The Reclamation of Mineral Workings (2006):

It is usually desirable to require that buildings, plant and machinery needed in connection with mineral working are removed as soon as they are no longer required in connection with the relevant planning permission. The areas concerned may then be incorporated in schemes for restoration and aftercare.

Modern gravel workings, therefore, can quickly 'disappear' from the landscape and what remains can quite easily be misinterpreted. The onus is thus on recording sites during the stages of operation and decommissioning. For older sites a range of evidence will need to be employed. This will include plans and descriptions of workings in planning permissions, where these survive, although they rarely record positions of plant. Ordnance Survey maps often record well-attested gravel workings, though neither systematically nor always accurately. Many sites can, of course, be identified superficially by remaining water elements, though it must always be remembered that many quarries operational from the 1960s onwards were at least partially restored to ground level, as described above. Aerial photographic evidence can be useful, particularly images specifically commissioned by operating companies which show sites during production. Very little photographic evidence of gravel quarries and plant on the ground has so far been archived, so investigators are very dependent on material in private hands, either those of operating companies or of former workers. Such material can be particularly valuable for understanding variations in methods of excavation, processing and transport relative to different operating companies, underlying geology, and changes in technology and over time. Most valuable are opportunities to visit both operating and redundant sites with those who have worked them, coupled with as great a range of the above types of evidence as possible.

Case study post-abandonment: Girton Quarry

During the course of conducting interviews for the present study, the opportunity arose for a site visit to early workings at Girton accompanied by a former employee of the gravel operator. Photographic evidence allowed conditions on the ground in January 2007 to be compared with the spatial relationship of production elements at points in the mid-1950s and mid-1960s.

Extraction of the high-quality gravel close to the Trent at Girton was commenced by 'Lincoln and Hull' in the early 1950s. The majority of output was transported by barge to Hull. In the early stages of working this was mainly in the form of raw material which was subsequently processed there and distributed to markets in the Humberside region. Figure 71, which shows operations c 1956, can be compared with Figure 72, which shows the same site in January 2007. Material was dug by dragline excavators from the wet pit visible in the foreground of Figure 71. At this time the pit covered an area of some 12ha and was being excavated from a waterside position roughly to the left of and behind the photographer. Excavated material was loaded straight into barges which were towed by diesel tug to the processing plant at the rear of the photograph.

Figure 71 Gravel working at Girton, 1956 (By courtesy of Dennis Thacker)

Figure 72 Viewpoint of Fig 71 in January 2007 (Photo: Tim Cooper/ARCUS)

Figure 73 Stockyard
of Girton Quarry,
1956 (By courtesy of
Dennis Thacker)

Figure 74 Viewpoint
of Fig 73 in January
2007, showing
remains of later
weighbridge (Photo:
Tim Cooper/
ARCUS)

At the pit-side wharf material was removed by grab cranes and fed onto conveyors for feeding to No. 1 plant (to the left of the photograph) and No. 2 plant (to the right). No. 1 plant was the first to be erected, in the early 1950s, and was essentially a large overhead hopper for storage of 'as dug' material which was taken by conveyor to a riverside wharf for loading on to barges (the wharf is out of view to the rear of the photograph). Material for processing was loaded by conveyor to No. 2 plant, which included machinery for crushing, washing, screening, and sand separation. Following processing it was delivered by another conveyor to storage hoppers from which manually operated chutes fed to dumptrucks for the transport of material to barges (via a riverside tipping ramp) or stockpiles. The majority of processed material also went by barge to Hull; the lorry discharge point for barge loading can just be seen in the background to the extreme right of the photograph.

Figure 73 shows the quarry stockyard, also in 1956. To the centre left of the photograph a Bedford lorry is being used to take material from storage bins to ground stockpiles. At the rear of the photograph are the site offices and weighbridge area. Figure 74 shows the same area in January 2007. Figure 75 shows the plant from across the pit that was being worked *c* 1965 and can be compared with the same view in January 2007 (Fig 76). No. 2 plant is visible at the centre rear of the photograph, with the crushing plant joined by conveyor to the right. Two Ruston Bucyrus 24 RB grab cranes can be seen removing material for loading to the plant. At this time a good deal of processed material was being sent by barge to a ready-mixed concrete plant at Castleford (now West Yorkshire). The quarry was taken over by Hoveringham Gravels in 1967 and subsequently by Tarmac which worked the site until 2000. Figure 77 shows a general view of the site with remnants of plant from this later period. A new Girton Quarry was opened by Tarmac at a site further away from the river in April 2005.

Figure 75 Girton Quarry, *c* 1965 (By courtesy of Dennis Thacker)

Figure 76 Viewpoint of Fig 75, with High Marnham power station in background (Photo Tim Cooper/ ARCUS)

Figure 77 Plant remains in January 2007 at the former Girton Quarry (closed 2000) with High Marnham (centre) and Cottam (right) power stations in the background. This area was infilled with PFA from High Marnham. (Photo: Tim Cooper/ ARCUS)

Case study during and post-operation: Hoveringham Quarry

The winding up of operations at Hoveringham during the course of the present study provided the opportunity for a case study in recording a quarry during the final phase of extraction and the start of decommissioning. Accordingly, site visits were made in September 2005 and September 2007, accompanied on both occasions by the operations area manager. Quarrying at Hoveringham has involved the extraction of sand and gravel from an area of some 500ha bounded to the north and south by the villages of Bleasby and Hoveringham, to the west by the Nottingham to Newark railway line, and to the east by the River Trent (Fig 78). At its peak, Hoveringham was the largest sand and gravel quarry in Nottinghamshire, with an annual production of over 500,000 tonnes of material.

Extraction commenced in September 1939 from land on the site of the later processing plant. In 1947 permission with limited conditions (Appendix 4) was granted for working to the immediate south of Bleasby (Areas 1, 2) following which natural regeneration to vegetation took place around the water-filled pits.[4] The Bleasby pits were worked as a separate quarry with its own processing plant until 1958, when the plant was dismantled and removed. A remaining small area in that vicinity was worked from Hoveringham Quarry in the late 1960s. Thirty years after initial extraction the lagoons were sold by the operating company to Bleasby parish council for a nominal sum to be used as a local amenity following additional planting. The site, known since restoration as Jubilee Ponds, is used in particular for fishing.

Area 3, to the north of and including the remaining lagoon, was worked from 1950 with no restoration conditions attached. The area to the immediate north of the lagoon, known by the company as 'Pit F', was subsequently filled with PFA and returned to agriculture. Permission was also granted in the early 1950s for the working of a large area immediately adjacent to the River Trent, just off the photograph to the right (Area 4). That part, known as 'Pit T', was also infilled with PFA and restored to agriculture. The remaining lagoons were converted for use by Nottinghamshire County Sailing Club. Extraction from these riverside areas ceased in 1963. Area 5 was granted consent in 1956 with conditions relating to the conservation of topsoil and overburden for re-use following infilling with 'waste-materials', in the event PFA. An adjacent area, the so-called Silt Ponds were subsequently restored as water amenities.

From the late 1960s quarrying was concentrated on two areas, with all of Area 6 and part of Area 7 being restored to agriculture with PFA, and the remaining part of Area 7, adjacent to the railway line, being given over to recreational fishing. The majority of working in these areas was finished by the late 1970s. From the time of the takeover of Hoveringham Gravels Ltd by Tarmac Roadstone in 1981, most of the working took place in an area bounded to the north by the road between Hoveringham and Thurgarton and to the west by the railway line (Area 8). At the same time, more limited working continued in the area next to the river in the vicinity of the 'sailing lakes'. The main area extended southwards until closure of the quarry in the summer of 2007, by which time it had been partially restored with PFA, leaving the remainder as a mixed amenity water restoration.

Figure 78 View north across main historic working area of Hoveringham Quarry, September 2001 (By courtesy of Tarmac Group)

Figure 79 Aerial view of main plant at Hoveringham Quarry, September 2001 (By courtesy of Tarmac Group)

Main plant

The main plant area of the quarry, as it appeared in September 2001, can be seen in Figure 79. The original plant was designed and built by the Robert Cort company of Reading and commenced production in September 1939 at a rate of 75 tons of processed material per hour. Figure 80 shows the modified plant still in production in September 2005. By this time the lorry loading bins visible in the centre of Figure 79 had been dismantled due to structural problems and a modified conveyor was delivering fully processed material to a ground stockpile. At the time that the aerial photograph (Fig 79) was taken, material as dug arrived at the plant on a field conveyor visible at the bottom left of the picture and was then conveyed to the plant for processing via two reclaim conveyors positioned over recovery tunnels (left of picture). Figure 81 shows the main plant in the process of demolition in September 2007.

Tipping shed

The area referred to as the 'tipping shed' was located next to the second conveyor from the left in the aerial photograph. Figure 82 shows the site in use in 1957 with a diesel loco and jubilee skips in position for tipping material into the recovery tunnel (see Chapter 2 and compare with Fig 40).

Workshops

The workshops and ancillary buildings at Hoveringham, visible on either side of the processing plant in Figure 79, were the most extensive of any sand and gravel quarry in the Trent Valley. By the 1950s almost all machinery used on site and at the company's other quarries was manufactured here on an assembly line located in the buildings with roof skylights to the bottom centre of the photograph. The adjacent buildings included workshops for welding, vehicle maintenance and repair, carpentry, and painting, as well as a pre-cast concrete and brick works. A separate Hoveringham Engineering Company was set up in 1957 for design and fabrication of steel structures for use in the mining and construction industries both in the UK and abroad. This company, which subsequently changed its name to Invicta Bridge Engineering, was later based at the right-hand end of the more recent workshops visible next to the processing plant in the aerial photograph. The left-hand end of these buildings was occupied by the static and mobile plant departments. Figure 83 shows the vehicle maintenance workshop awaiting demolition in September 2007.

Figure 80
Main plant at Hoveringham Quarry, September 2005. A modified delivery conveyor i forming a stockpile of 2/40 mm gravel on a site formerly occupied by storage hoppers, removed after 2001 (compar Fig 79). Otherwise, this structure is recognisably that first erected in the 1940s (see Fig 49) (Photo: Tim Coope ARCUS)

Offices and canteen

The rapid expansion of Hoveringham Gravels also meant that it was one of the first companies to incorporate clerical, technical and associated buildings on its main site. By the mid-1950s these were housed in a building equipped with a large drawing office, accounting department and canteen for office and works personnel. This can be seen adjacent to the pond at the bottom of Figure 79. Following Hoveringham's change of status to a public company in 1963 a state of-the-art concrete office block and corporate headquarters was built at a cost of over £200,000 (to the lower right of Fig 79). Opened in 1965 by Lord 'RAB' Butler as Master of Trinity College Cambridge, the landowners, this was of a two-storey design intended to fit appropriately into its rural setting and provide accommodation for around 200 personnel. The reinforced concrete frame incorporated exposed aggregate panels and local cobbles in various colours, while the suspended ceiling in the entrance hall consisted of a low-relief plaster sculpture on the theme of prehistoric geology, the work of local artist Kim James, who was also responsible for a striking sculpture of a mammoth in stainless steel that graced the outside of the building (Fig 84).

Former company employees remember the buildings with affection: the plush carpeting, the refrigerators and drinks cabinets in executive offices, the ultra-modern computer suite at the top of the building and the striking display boards in the foyer with pictures of the company's characteristic orange vehicles being loaded with gravel. Following Hoveringham Gravels' acquisition by Tarmac Roadstone in 1981 the offices fell quickly into disuse (Fig 85). Just how quickly is vividly recalled by former employee Tom Dodsley:

> I think the offices were actually closed by the Christmas holiday, and I went in the canteen shortly after and it was a bit like the *Marie Celeste*, where people had just gone and left it – there were knives and forks still set at the tables, crockery and beakers with the Hoveringham Mammoth on the side – it was amazing!

By 1990 the mammoth sculpture had been moved to a site at Nottingham Trent University, a gift of the Tarmac company, the later operator of the site, and in April 2008 the office buildings were demolished. Just how quickly the history of an aggregates company even of the significance of Hoveringham can be lost is highlighted by the Public Monument and Sculpture Association's catalogue entry for the mammoth sculpture. Noting its current location, the catalogue suggests that the subject of the sculpture was chosen on the grounds that 'remains of this animal were perhaps discovered during construction of the [university] building'; the association with the once-famous Hoveringham Company was already forgotten.

Figure 82 The 'tipping shed' at Hoveringham Quarry, 1957 (By courtesy of QMJ Publishing Ltd)

Figure 83 Newly built offices and company headquarters of Hoveringham Gravels Ltd, complete with 'mammoth' sculpture, 1964 (By courtesy of Nigel Hunt)

Figure 84 Exterior
view of workshops
at Hoveringham
awaiting demolition,
September 2007
(Photo: Tim Cooper/
ARCUS)

Figure 85 Canteen
at Hoveringham
Quarry, September
2007. Compare with
same viewpoint,
Fig 93 (Photo: Tim
Cooper/ARCUS)

Notes

1   ie evenly shaped rounded quartzite, an excellent concreting aggregate.

2   Geodiversity is defined by the UKRIGS Geoconservation Association as 'the variety of rocks, fossils and minerals and natural processes' citing Prosser, C (2002) in 'Terms of endearment' *Earth Heritage* (17), 12–13

3   I am grateful to Mr Tom White of Durham University for information on antiquarians working in the Trent Valley and for his transcript of AL Armstrong's notes.

4   The decription of phased working from Hoveringham Quarry is based on a document in the possession of the Tarmac Group. I am grateful to the company for their loan of this and other materials during the course of my research.

✎ FOUR ✎

People

Recruitment and jobs

The Trent Valley in which the sand and gravel industry developed during the course of the 20th century was essentially an agricultural region which, unlike the neighbouring Peak District, for example, had no tradition of mining or quarrying on anything more than a small scale. The early development of the industry, as an extension of river working, was part of this rural scene. It is unsurprising, therefore, that the emergence of quarrying on an increasingly industrial scale, in the period up to and including the Second World War, had an impact on communities in the region.

Tensions were exacerbated by the fact that the emerging industry did not bring workers from outside but drew on the labour of sons, and occasionally daughters, of farmers, who would traditionally have been destined for a lifetime in agriculture. More than anything, it was the inability of farmers to compete with the wages on offer in the emerging industry that caused ill-feeling, a situation only worsened by the shortage of labour caused by the onset of war. Many farmers hoped that the growing number of gravel pits of the 1940s would be simply a passing fad, providing temporary employment to satisfy the war effort. Deg Bellamy, himself brought up in the Nottinghamshire farming community of Brough, laughs as he remembers considering his first job at the age of fourteen: 'When I left school there was a farmer in the village who said, at the time that Besthorpe pit was opened, "Don't go down there to work because it will all be finished after the war".'

Born ten years later, in 1939, Dennis Thacker started work on a local farm at the age of sixteen but soon left to work at the local gravel pit which had the same appeal of outdoor work but brought home between £6 and £8 a week instead of £3. The fact that it involved some 30 hours a week in overtime was no barrier to those brought up to the long hours of agricultural work. Like many young people who traded farming for quarrying, it was when he saw the plant at work across neighbouring fields that he decided to make the switch. Bryan Atkin grew up next to the gravel pit at Acton, which had been part of the Mainwaring estate for over 150 years:

> I started off in agriculture, and went to agricultural college, but I needed more money to buy a house so I went into HGV driving. My father lived at Acton from 1949. He was one of three or four tenants and farmed 500 acres of the estate, a mixed farm. When I helped him during the holidays I would sometimes be in the field next to the quarry and would be attracted to it because I was interested in machines. It was better paid than agricultural work and you got a lot of agricultural

workers coming into the industry. They made good quarry workers because they were similar environments – hard work, outdoors.

Barry Hulland worked on local farms in his native village of Longford, Derbyshire, from the age of eleven before taking a full-time job as soon as he left school at fourteen. He, too, soon made the switch to lorry driving and then gravel working and supports the view that farm workers were temperamentally suited to quarrying. In fact, in his later role as a quarry manager he specifically targeted them:

> The quarry lads who have been in it any length of time are a breed unto themselves! If there was a vacancy I used to look for an ex-farmer because they seemed to be more willing, they didn't care what they did, what the weather was when they were doing it or what time they finished at night – within reason!

Up until quite recent times it was not uncommon for men to combine quarrying with agricultural work. Deg Bellamy's wife remembers how, before they were married, he would do an hour chopping beet and would still get to work for six in the morning. In the summer months he would start his work on the land at four. In the evening, according to his wife, they would 'go out dancing until the early hours and he'd still be at work early!' At Hilton, where the local squire, James Marston Spurrier, also owned the gravel pit, the workforce would be shared between quarry and estate. When he needed work doing in the fields Spurrier would send a lorry to fetch men from the pit and to take them back later. In this way, according to Terry Cliff, 'I worked quite a long time on the farm even though I was being paid by Hilton Gravel.' Terry also points to the fact that many people in the industry got their first jobs through knowing, or more often actually being related to, existing workers:

Figure 86 Trent Gravels' worker known as 'Blowpipe' in recognition of his job of pumping cement into the batching plant at Attenborough, *c* 1955 (By courtesy of Michael Arthur)

> If you go through the Hilton Gravel quarries you will see that there were often family connections; at Hilton there was me, Uncle George, Uncle Harry, Uncle Bill, my Granddad and even Pauline [his wife] worked for BCA in the office for a time, so that was five of us working for the same company! At Mercaston there was the Wards, the Booths and the Coldwells; at Hemington there was the Fairbrothers and others.

Dorothy Winn (née Scrivener) was another person from a rural background who got work in the industry through a relative. She started in a clerical position at Hoveringham Quarry in 1946:

> My brother, Robert, had been working there since it started in 1939. On one occasion he came home on leave [from National Service] and I'd just had two years at technical college and had taken a job in Nottingham. But coming from a little village like Thurgarton, I didn't like working in town. Robert went down to Hoveringham and the lad in the office had been called up into the forces and Mr North [the quarry manager] asked my brother whether he knew of anybody who would like a job there. He said that he did and got me an appointment; I gave my notice in and started about a week later.

Many quarry workers look back on a time when their workmates were their neighbours, or relatives, and have noticed a change from a position in which many co-workers lived in the village to one where they could no longer afford to. According to Barry Hulland, who swapped farming for quarrying, this was a situation paralleled by changes within agriculture itself:

> I came from an agricultural family, but farming at that time [the 1960s] was starting to go downhill; smaller farms were being sold to make the larger ones that we have today and so there was no opportunity to have your own farm. At that time I lived in Longford which is right out in the country. This is where I had been born; it was all agriculture in my day but now the houses have been taken over by business people – there's only about two families left that were there in my day.

By the immediate post-war period, despite the industry's relatively recent origins, a clear hierarchy of management, staff, and workers was visible at most Trent Valley gravel pits. At its base were the 'unskilled' labourers employed in tasks such as monitoring the operation of conveyors, cleaning up material that had fallen off, and generally helping to maintain the site in a relatively clean, workable condition. Next came the 'skilled' workforce, the first rung of which consisted of the loco, lorry, and truck drivers, followed by the operators of mechanical shovels and dumpers. At the top of the workforce pyramid were the mechanical excavator drivers, crane drivers, suction pump and dredger operators, and the ubiquitous fitters, without whom production would often have ground to a halt. At the bottom of the so-called 'staff' levels were the foreman and the office and weighbridge clerks, who, in turn, supported the quarry manager and his immediate clerical staff. In all, the size of the workforce generally varied between the nine men who worked the sandstone at Acton to the 40 or so who worked the Trent Valley's first 'super-pit' at Hoveringham.

Whether workers stuck to a single job, or were rotated, depended mainly on the staffing needs of individual quarries. At Hoveringham, whose company structure allowed for high staffing levels, people tended to be kept to a single job. Within a smaller workforce, such as at Acton,

> everyone had specific jobs but there were also communal jobs such as watching the conveyors and cleaning up. You came in at the bottom and did a bit of everything to learn the trade and then would be established as the fitter, the dozer driver, the weighbridge clerk or whatever, but you could interchange.
>
> *(Bryan Atkin)*

In the early days of the industry, at least, it was not just the manual workers who were expected to undertake multiple tasks. Dorothy Winn was in charge of the office at Hoveringham during a very busy period in the early 1950s:

> My job was classed as 'weighbridge clerk' but I had to check the wages, the drivers' time sheets, nearly everything because I was the only one in the office then. By the end of the day I'd have a big sheet and you had to write down the tonnage of

everything that had gone out and what type of material it was, and I had to add up all these columns in my head. That was before they got the adding machine. Later they took on two more girls, one to operate the adding machine. During my time they got their first fleet of lorries and I had to get all the drivers' measurements and order overalls.

Pay and hours

The first general wage agreement across the industry in the Midlands region was implemented in 1939 following negotiations involving the National Union of General and Municipal Workers (GMWU) and the Transport and General Workers' Union (TGWU). On the employers' side, signatories included Branston Gravels Ltd, Burton and Branston Sand and Gravel Co Ltd, Derbyshire Gravel & Aggregates Ltd (Repton), Hilton Gravel Ltd, Stenson Gravel Co Ltd (Barrow-on-Trent), Trent Gravels Ltd (Attenborough), and Willington Gravels Ltd of Egginton. At the same time the parties agreed the constitution of a new conciliation board to determine future wages, hours and working conditions for the industry (National Archives LAB 83/160). The wages and terms were set as follows:

Labourers, including Narrow Gauge Loco Drivers, Tug Boat Drivers:

Unskilled (over 21) 1s 1d per hour

Skilled (over 21) 1s 2d per hour

Driver, Chase Side Shovel and Dumper, over 21: 1s 2½d per hour

Driver, Mechanical Excavator (inc Shovel, Skimmer, Scoop, Dragline, Back Trencher), over 21: 1s 4d per hour

Driver, Crane, over 21: 1s 4d per hour

Pump Man, Pontoon, over 21: 1s 4d per hour

Workers under 21 years of age:

Age 14: 3¾d per hour

Age 15: 4d per hour

Age 16: 4½d per hour

Age 17: 6d per hour

Age 18: 8d per hour

Age 19: 9¼d per hour

Age 20: 10½d per hour

Conditions

Hours of Work

The basic principle is that of a 48 hour week exclusive of Saturday afternoons and Sundays, to be interpreted in the Winter season (1st October to end February) as 46 hours and in the Summer season (1st March to 30th September) as 50 hours

Overtime

Overtime shall be paid at the rate of time and a quarter for all time worked over the above stipulated week

Holidays

Twelve days' holiday (including the six statutory days' holiday), the other six being given consecutively, shall be paid for each 12 months' employment

An agreement in 1955 saw the main wage bracket rise to 3s 2d per hour and in 1969 it rose to twice this level. On this occasion the agreement between SAGA and the unions included the standardisation of a 40-hour week throughout the year, to be worked over five- or five and a half-day weeks. Overtime worked on weekdays, including Saturdays, was to be calculated on a daily basis after the normal number of hours had been worked each day. The rate for the first two hours was to be time and a third and after that, time and a half. All time worked on Sundays, whether for maintenance, repairs, or actual production was to be paid at double time. Night shift pay, where applicable, was to be paid at 6d above basic rate. There was occasionally the need for unscheduled overtime (Fig 87).

It was the sheer number of hours available to be worked in gravel quarrying that made the main difference to levels of remuneration in the industry. Many employees worked seven days a week in the high-production days of the 1950s and 1960s and, with treble pay available from some companies on Bank Holidays, gave up the majority of their time to the job. Terry Cliff was working as a lorry driver for Hilton Gravels in the early 1960s:

> I would have to do an eleven-hour day to make a reasonable wage, from 7 in the morning to 6 in the evening, 7 to 4 on a Saturday delivering in the morning, washing down and greasing in the afternoon. You were responsible for all your own vehicle maintenance. If you were lucky enough to get a load on Saturday afternoon you could then go in for four hours on a Sunday morning to carry out your maintenance and you would get double-time.

Tom Dodsley remembers a particularly punctilious excavator driver when he was in charge at Hoveringham Quarry: 'he was never absent and worked seven days a week, 6 till 6, 6 till 4 on a Saturday and 8 till 4 on a Sunday. Eventually he had to be cut down to six days; this was not at all unusual in those days.' The situation of production going all out to meet demand was common to quarries all along of the Trent Valley between the 1950s and 1970s:

> The early days at Hoveringham were so busy that it was taken for granted that people would stay on and do what was necessary. If there was an emergency and someone needed more gravel I would have to stop on to get the lorries out.

Sometimes I'd be there twelve hours; it was just taken for granted that you would stay. (Dorothy Winn)

People would work twelve-hour days. Then at times it was really busy and demand soared so they introduced a shift system. I worked seven days a week for years. (Deg Bellamy)

The conveyors would be run on a Sunday, especially during busy periods, and the only time to do maintenance was on a Saturday afternoon or a Sunday. Hoveringham worked seven days a week to make up for stoppages on the conveyors; 'the plant would beat the conveyors' and so weekends would be used for catching up. (Tom Dodsley)

Routine maintenance would take place on Saturday afternoon and Sunday morning. Saturday afternoon was usually optional, but you were in your twenties and needed the money. You weren't expected to work every weekend but it was frowned upon if you did not pull your weight. There were some people who liked to 'live' there. (Bryan Atkin)

In recent years the trend has been towards more conventional working hours and annual salaries. In 2005 a typical contract would be worked on the basis of an average 48-hour week with six weeks' leave per year. According to Gary Pell, who at that time was Assistant Quarry Manager (AQM) at Attenborough:

Everyone can now make a decent living without having to do all the overtime available. The company does not say that you must do 48 hours a week; you will do whatever the manager deems necessary for that particular week or day, they don't stand on hours. You'll never do that many hours in a year and if you do 60 hours one week you'll do 20 the next.

In many companies the change has been symbolised by the move away from a clocking-on culture which prevailed throughout most of the industry. When Mick Turner took over operations at Attenborough in 1994,

Figure 87 Hilton Gravel workers help to rescue a Derby Airlines DC3 airliner which had overshot the runway of Burnaston airport, early 1960s (By courtesy of *Derby Evening Telegraph*)

The first thing I did was take the clocking-in machine off the wall and throw it in the dustbin. I thought there would be a round of applause but actually they liked it because they knew where they stood. But they needed to produce from 7 in the morning to 5 in the evening and I didn't need a clocking-in machine to make that happen. If they don't need to be here at 4.30 then let them go home, but if they need to be here at 5.30 they should still be here. But they used to be hanging round the machine at 4.30.

To a large extent, inevitably, the rise of wage rates in the industry has been at the expense of the size of the workforce, which is now about half what it was in most quarries 20 years ago. A fairly typical situation was the quarry where

There were 39 on the clock when my friend had worked there; when I went there fifteen years later [as manager] there were fifteen lads and when I finished I had eleven, so they even cut me down, though salaries were going up. (Barry Hulland)

Working conditions

In the pre-mechanised era, in particular, gravel working had much in common with the outdoor working environment of other forms of quarrying. Some jobs were certainly physically demanding. At sites such as Girton, Hilton, and Hoveringham, where excavated material was loaded onto wagons and taken to the plant by diesel locos, one of the hardest jobs was that of the 'tipping shed operative' who had to discharge the material by hand into the receiving hoppers. After tipping the material, the man would have to break up and remove big lumps

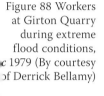

Figure 88 Workers at Girton Quarry during extreme flood conditions, c 1979 (By courtesy of Derrick Bellamy)

from the grid on top of the hopper before another load could be discharged. However, gravel workers generally agree that their working conditions were less arduous than those of the hard rock quarrymen. As for the outdoor nature of the job, for all workers this was a necessary condition and for most, a positive attraction:

> There was no question that you would do your work in the pouring rain, the sleet, and the snow; you carried on. That was the biggest shock I had coming into this industry. In other types of outdoor work I had done, when it tipped it down you stopped and got in the van; with this you got going. (Mick Turner)

> Most breakdowns occur in the cold and wet so you're out there in the cold in this industry more than you are in the summer; in the summer you're dressed up in all this gear and sweating. (Gary Pell)

> It was fun! Every job is what you make it – this is an outside job, if you're going to get wet you're going to get wet, so what? (Barry Hulland)

More serious challenges came with the frequent flooding which was a feature of river terrace pits (Figs 88–89). Workers who lived on the west bank of the Trent would cross the river to work at Girton by sculling a small 'cog' boat, which became something more of a test during severe flooding, such as occurred following the harsh winter of 1947. Deg Bellamy remembers his foreman, Durgin Thornhill, attempting the crossing once on a high river when the wind was whipping the surface into waves, and seeing him being blown almost out of sight down the river before he managed to land on the other side. On another occasion, when the Trent had risen above the level of the hedges in the riverside fields, Durgin was asked by the other men in the boat what would happen when they got over the gravel pit, which was then at a depth of 40 feet: 'We could drown here where it's ten feet just as easily as over the pit where it's forty' came the deadpan reply. Deg Bellamy's wife was one of many who worried when the men were out on the swollen river in those days without any safety gear.

Further upstream the river might have been less expansive but it became just as hazardous, to both men and machines, when it went into flood. Terry Cliff remembers an occasion at Repton in the early 1970s when the river suddenly burst its banks: 'The men on top of the plant could see it about to happen and called out. They had put a 72 RB [excavator] up on a temporary bank to keep it out of the water. The next morning all you could see was the jib sticking up; it took six months to get it running again.' Flooding presented continual production problems at riverside pits. The incident with the excavator was part of an ongoing struggle to win gravel at Repton, as recalled by Barry Hulland:

> At Repton we had to get up in eight months what you would normally produce in twelve because of the floods, so in summertime you would be working flat out to get a quantity up. Every year you would lose six weeks to flooding and would have to produce from the surge pile. You'd often have everything pumped out and then a week later you'd be underwater again. It was very depressing but you're not allowed to put up banks to prevent it as that would flood Willington village.

Figure 89 Ruston
Bucyrus dragline
excavator stranded
during flooding at
Girton, 1950s (By
courtesy of Dennis
Thacker)

Equally incapacitating were the frozen winter conditions in which production would literally seize up (Fig 90). An older generation of gravel workers have memories of walking across a frozen Trent in 1932 and of wondering if they would ever be able to dig gravel again in 1947. During the prolonged freezing weather of 1963 workers at Girton had to break through ice almost 30cm thick with dynamite, and at Attenborough ice was still being found in the gravel stockpiles in June. In the words of Barry Hulland, who worked at, and subsequently managed, Repton Quarry:

> There was not a lot you could do when things were frozen up. If it was extreme they would put you down to 40 hours [a week], but no-one was really bothered because there was nothing you could do. You would know the temperature at which the plant would still be able to operate; so, for example, Repton could be run at -4 frost. In the morning you would look at the thermometer in the tree; if it was below 4, forget it, because you knew the pumps would be frozen and you would create a lot of expense by trying to produce because of breakages of belts, pumps and so on. But everywhere was different and you'd get to know the 'level' of each plant. Hemington was terrible because it was very exposed and you wouldn't be able to produce at -3. The plants use a lot of water so when you drained off at night you could easily get a lot of icicles in the morning.

The main decision that had to be made by foremen and managers was whether plant could be operated safely and profitably. According to Deg Bellamy, who went to work at Girton in the early 1960s, the different attitudes of operating companies were highlighted during harsh winter conditions:

> With 'Lincoln and Hull' – where it was their boats that fetched the material, their plant, everything was theirs – you had to keep the conveyors moving so they didn't freeze and break. They'd let you work weekends so that it would be going on Monday morning. But the other [companies] wouldn't; you'd be struggling on Monday morning to get it going.

Figure 90 Frozen
plant at Hemington,
c 1982 (By courtesy
of Barry Hulland)

One of the main considerations involved in a decision to carry on producing
was the personal safety of the workers. Fortunately, few in the industry witnessed
serious accidents and fatalities at first hand. Where accidents did occur they
usually involved a hazardous combination of a highly mechanised working
environment and a willingness to compromise safety in the pursuit of productivity.
Dorothy Winn reflects on attitudes at Hoveringham Quarry just after the war:
'There weren't really a lot of *serious* accidents. My brother had his leg broken by
a dumper bucket; they were the kind of accidents that would not have happened
if people had abided by the rules. People did it to get jobs done quickly.'

Probably the greatest single cause of serious injury, and worse, was falling
from moving vehicles. Jack Thornhill remembers the old Muir-Hill dumpers
used for muck shifting, with such a narrow wheelbase that they would 'tip over
on a molehill' (Fig 91). So common were accidents involving dumpers at Girton
Quarry in the 1950s that on one occasion, when informed that a machine had
been lost down a hole the response of the foreman was: 'Ne'er mind, go and fetch
another one from the shed.' More seriously, Jack remembers the dangers involved
in dumping material on top of overburden mounds at Girton:

> There was a fatal accident with a dumper going over the top of the spoil heap and
> the driver being drowned. Another driver went over with a dumper but managed
> to get out before it hit the water. Not many men who drove those dumpers didn't
> end up in the water at some point.

Trent Valley gravel workers during the production boom years of the 1950s
remember this as a time when unannounced visits by Health and Safety inspectors
became more frequent. On the first occasion this happened at Hoveringham

Quarry, Dorothy Winn, who was in charge of the office, had to admit that she did not know where the accident book was kept. Working environment legislation, of which the Mines and Quarries Act of 1954 was a particular milestone, was starting to be introduced throughout industry. The subsequent introduction of the Notification of Dangerous Occurrences Order in 1962 made it more difficult for employers to turn a blind eye to dangerous practices. Increasing attention by government to the working environment in general culminated in the introduction of the Health and Safety at Work Act in 1974, which, in its subsequent amendments, governs conditions in the modern workplace. Against the background of an increase in serious accidents across the quarrying sector in the early 1980s, the 1990s saw increasing insistence by the government's Health and Safety Executive (HSE) that the industry set its house in order. It was then apparent that, as in other areas of employment, a shift in workplace culture would be required if the situation were to be dealt with once and for all. Mick Turner, who became manager at Attenborough in 1994, was particularly determined to tackle the borderline area between what some might consider acceptable camaraderie and others would deem a dangerously 'macho' culture:

In my time I have never come across a fatal accident, but loads of scuffed fingers, broken bones, blood pouring out and so on. And a lot of it was part of the image: 'Hey, we're quarrymen we are!' When I took over, five of the men had fingers missing. Invariably it is people's behaviour that causes accidents. It took ten years to get people wearing hard hats but now it's second nature. There was a lot of the 'you work hard and you play hard' macho behaviour – 'you can get on that grizzly feeder and get that rock off, no problem, you're a quarryman!' – and it was no different in sand and gravel from hard rock: 'It's a man's game, you're bound to lose a finger in this job aren't you?'. I mean, 20 years ago there were still initiation rites.

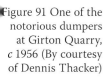

Figure 91 One of the notorious dumpers at Girton Quarry, *c* 1956 (By courtesy of Dennis Thacker)

The other shift in attitudes that has occurred over the past 30 years has been on the management side and was witnessed first hand by Tom Dodsley in his capacity as an area manager:

There were occasional accidents; I can remember two in particular. One was at Newark where a man was buried by material coming out of a hopper and killed, and one at Hoveringham where... [pause]. The one at Newark shouldn't happen any more because of modern Health and Safety procedures such as structural inspections. Accidents nowadays are more behavioural. The incident at Hoveringham when I was manager was very nasty. The man had removed the guard from a running conveyor and was trying to clean at the back of a drum and got his overalls caught between the belt and the drum and his arm was badly injured. In the old days such accidents would have been seen as acceptable, as part of the job. Nowadays disciplinary action would probably be taken against people working against instructions. Production no longer takes priority over safety.

The quarrying industry as a whole now views Health and Safety as a top priority, as evidenced by the launch of the 'Hard Target' initiative by its representative body, the Quarry Products Association (QPA), in 2000. This followed the introduction of new Quarries Regulations by the HSE in 1999 which placed particular emphasis on the use of personal protective equipment (PPE) such as reflective clothing, hard hats, ear protectors, and protective eye-wear. Use of machinery is now regulated by dual key procedures and quarries are regularly monitored for dust and noise levels. In general, the industry is considerably more open to the sharing of best practice. Attenborough is a good case in point. In the ten years to 2005 the site's health and safety record showed a marked improvement, in recognition of which it collected a number of industry awards. According to manager Mick Turner, the introduction of NVQ qualifications in Health and Safety and Continued Professional Development schemes 'have helped bring the quarry industry into the modern world'.

Particularly noticeable have been the improvements that have been made to vehicle safety, which includes the introduction of features such as grab-rails, reversing sirens, and driver's cameras (Fig 92). Ken Bagnall witnessed the changes during many years as a bulldozer driver at Acton: 'During that time the main improvement in the machinery was in terms of comfort. You started to get air-conditioning ... and doors that shut properly!' Gary Pell at Attenborough is also half-joking when he comments that 'They're spoiling people a bit these days, putting air-conditioning, heated screens and so on into machines – you get the lot now!'

However, quarry workers were arguably never so spoilt as in the days that Hoveringham Gravels operated its own on-site catering facilities (Fig 93). The building in which they were housed became redundant when the company was taken over in 1981. Peering inside in 2005, former manager Tom Dodsley recalled the old arrangements with barely concealed nostalgia:

Figure 92 An
interesting incident
outside the Theatre
Royal, Nottingham,
early 1960s; more
vehicles meant
more accidents
(By courtesy of G
Campbell)

There were three canteens in there; Hoveringham used to do things in a way that
we just don't do them nowadays. There was a workman's canteen for the lads off
the quarry, the drivers, and the chaps from the fitting sheds and then there was
one for the staff and another for the managers.

Despite the evident hierarchical system that was in place, former office worker
Dorothy Winn is quick to point out that the workers got bigger portions of food
than the 'staff' like herself. Dorothy's daughter, Angela, ended up working in the
canteen: 'We prepared an elaborate three-course menu for all the workers, who
would take an hour off. Those who couldn't get away, such as the weighbridge
people, would have it taken on a tray.'

Pearl Michael (see Fig 93), who ran the canteen and was interviewed for the
company newspaper in 1971, clearly evokes the benign paternalism of a family-
run business from a bygone era of heavy industry:

We do like to put on dishes that are a bit unusual. We had prawn curry on Monday.
Today we've had Spaghetti Florentine with Crispy Bacon, and tomorrow we've got
spiced pork with apricots and fried rice. I remember first putting on a dish called
Gnocchi as the 'B' lunch – usually the 'A' lunch attracts 85% of the trade because
it's a standard sort of meal. The first time we cooked *Gnocchi* we had three people
for it. I think anyone, even in the trade, would find it difficult to believe that we
now get more for it than for the 'A' lunch; indeed, it's the only 'B' meal that can
outstrip the 'A'.

Figure 93
Canteen staff at
Hoveringham
Quarry prepare a
giant Christmas
pudding, 1977.
Company Catering
Manager, Miss
Pearl Michael, is
second from right
(By courtesy of
Tarmac Group)

Mechanisation and automation

The transformation from a job that involved hard physical work to one that was more a case of men monitoring machines was a key feature of the development of the aggregates industry from the 1950s onwards. As with most technological developments of modern industry, the lead was taken in the United States, and in this country quarry managers looked on enviously at the 'push-button quarries' that were appearing in places like Idaho and Ohio. An article in the trade press in 1957 predicted a Brave New World of 'Line upon line of machines in continuous automatic production. Men only supervise, change tools and maintain. No longer do they operate.' Whilst acknowledging that for workers in the industry automation was a 'fearful word', the author argued that its benefits were clear in enabling Britain to leap forward to a standard of living 'that would have seemed incredible to our immediate ancestors'. People would not disappear from the scene completely, however:

> Redundancy of labour can never happen in the quarrying industry except in the rare instance that a quarry ceases to operate. Nor, unfortunately, can the industry have complete automation ... quarrying practice must always remain a matter of human control. Every situation is in some way different from all others ever experienced in quarrying and no electronic brain could ever be trusted to direct operations.
>
> (*Quarry Management and Products*, November 1957, p 124).

In reality, both automation and mechanisation led directly to redundancy on a large scale and within ten years of this prediction the director of the Institute of Quarrying was admitting that by means of '... rapid progress towards complete mechanisation ... the steady increase in total annual production has been accompanied by an equally steady fall in the number of personnel required.' As for 'electronic brains', the application of digital technology to quarrying, a process which began in the 1960s, now goes as far as monitoring barge movements at Attenborough by a satellite navigation system. Inevitably, it was the unskilled section of the workforce, such as the men who would remove lumps of clay from conveyors (Fig 94), that took the full brunt of the move towards mechanisation. However, by the start of the 21st century developments in design and technology had brought changes across the board. At Attenborough, for instance:

> There's no-one on a clay-picking belt now because it's been mechanised, they've 'grizzlied' [screened] it off at the face with a mechanical picker. At the end of the day, we have made things a lot better for ourselves and that's got to be technology and forward-thinking managers, not those that have been left in the past ... Six people on [boats] was wasting time, lots of waiting to load or unload, only bringing 50 or 70 tonnes up. This was replaced by three tugs and barges and four dumb barges and we got more loads doing it that way and we lost three people – unfortunate, but that's the way of the world. (Mick Turner)

The relentless pace of mechanisation has also meant that the sand and gravel industry has provided a wealth of opportunities for fitters, and many quarry workers who started on general jobs ended up in this trade. Their job, supporting each phase of production – excavation, transport, and processing – might be seen as less technical than some in other sectors of industry, but has been no less essential. According to Gary Pell at Attenborough, who started out in this line of work: 'You're definitely a fitter in this industry, you're not a mechanic; it's all steel and welding, you're more of a fabricator. If there are jobs that are beyond your capabilities then we get contractors in.' Barry Hulland is another whose route into management came via work as a fitter:

> The job is very varied because you have got to repair things when they break but also try and prevent them from breaking in the first place. You can tell when things are going wrong by ear, you get to know the sound of everything, especially when screens are about to go. The different bearings make different whining noises and you know that inner bearings will fail within eight hours, an outer one you can run for eight months and the middle one makes a more piercing sound. If you heard a bearing at seven in the morning and it hadn't got any worse by nine then you knew that you hadn't got a problem; if it had got worse you'd get your spanners out because you knew that by lunchtime you'd be stripping it. So the job is everything really from repairing belts to fitting bearings, and dealing with whatever crushers you've got, which are always very labour-intensive. It was the variation that I liked about the job; everything from welding to fabrication work and so on.

Much of the value attached to fitters in the gravel industry derives from the abrasive nature of the material. Machinery and parts wear out relatively quickly and frequently, a situation that particularly applied before the recent replacement of steel screening mesh, for example, with compounds of nylon, plastic, and rubber. Overall, the contribution of mechanisation to the gravel industry is neatly summed up by Gary Pell, AQM at Attenborough:

> It could be the end of an era. There is a lot less manpower. For example, 20 years ago there used to be four men employed here whose job it was every day to clean up with shovels under the conveyor belts; now these have rubber skirts attached so material doesn't drop off. Now there are twelve men in total when production is going on. You used to have five men down at the dig, now there's only two. Technology has taken over from the manpower; it's brilliant. But look what it's done ...

Industrial relations

Unlike its big brother, coal, the quarrying industry was too widely dispersed and disparate in its organisational structure to become heavily unionised. In the sand and gravel sector, matters of pay, working conditions, and arbitration were all dealt with reasonably successfully by delegations from SAGA and the two main unions, the GMWU and the TGWU. In practice, the large companies such as Blue Circle operated a closed shop with the TGWU, although at companies that were more tolerant of plurality of representation, for example ARC, other unions, such as the Boiler Makers, occasionally got a foot in the door. Elsewhere, as at Hilton Gravels, a company established by the local landowner, union membership was actively discouraged: it was 'a taboo subject'. At Hoveringham, in the early days at least, according to Dorothy Winn, 'You weren't allowed to join a union but one or two did on the quiet. If it got around that you were a union person you lost your job.'

In those quarries where unions did manage to get something of a foothold, it was the TGWU that was most strongly represented, though not always with the full support of its members. Deg Bellamy rose to the position of foreman during his time at Besthorpe:

> Apart from me they were all members of a union and in the 70s there was a strike for six weeks. They were in the TGWU and they wanted to change to some other union but by law they couldn't. I said I wouldn't support a strike on that basis. They were picketing at 7.00, so the manager used to say to me 'come at 6'! They used to go home at 3.30 and I never saw them but they played hell with me when they saw me subsequently! But they were mostly good lads and I made up with them in time.

Former Trent Valley gravel workers are often quick to point out that on the few occasions that industrial unrest did break out, it was 'outside forces' that were to blame. Barry Hulland and Terry Cliff, who both worked at Derbyshire pits, remember one particular occasion:

> Barry: There were strikes in the 1970s – it was always the 'Birmingham' people!

They picketed us at Repton but we just went in on the footpaths. We all went to work and everyone was happy to do that, it was just lorry drivers like Terry [Cliff] that wouldn't come in.

Terry: There weren't strikes at Hilton Gravel but at BCA we once came out for three days, but that was a dispute in the West Midlands and the TGWU called everyone out. I think it was a dispute about the use of contractors. The picketing wasn't very seriously implemented; it was all thrashed out by the company and everyone went back to work as if nothing had happened. They were a good company like that.

Despite, or perhaps because of, the official bar on union membership at Hoveringham, unrest did occasionally spill over. Dorothy Winn had worked at the plant immediately after the war and, in later years, the family was represented there by her brother and son:

You had odd times when there were flare-ups with the workers, there were strikes. Our son David was in one, it would have been the early 70s, and my brother Bob. I think that they had one that lasted nearly nine weeks. When they went back a lot of men lost their jobs. It would have been over pay; there were pickets every day trying to stop lorries going in.

However, all former Hoveringham employees interviewed agree that the paternalistic nature of the company was generally benign, and in the long-run workers appreciated benefits such as the social and catering facilities and a generous pension scheme that were the trappings of a successful family-run public company.

Training and workforce development

It was a sign of how far the industry had come in a relatively short time that by the late 1950s companies were considering the best means of introducing formal training into their procedures. To a certain extent developments were precipitated by the implementation of the Mines and Quarries Act of 1954. For the first time, working practices that had developed in a more or less haphazard manner came under scrutiny at the highest level. The industry response was to join in discussions with government, educational bodies, and the trades unions, resulting in the formulation of City and Guilds training courses available at three levels, ranging from a general course aimed at operatives to an Advanced Certificate for managers and potential managers. Throughout all three schemes particular attention was to be given to safe working methods and the importance of accident prevention. Implementation for Midlands workers was to be focused on technical colleges at Buxton, Grantham, and Doncaster.

Mike Arthur, then working as a laboratory technician at Attenborough, was one of the first intake on the Sand, Gravel and Quarrying Certificate course at Grantham. In the wake of the implementation of the Industrial Training Act in 1964, Mike was then appointed as Company Training Officer by Trent Gravels in 1967, one of the first such posts to be created in the aggregates industry. The records generated from his time in the post provide a unique insight into the situation relative to training and workforce development in one of the longest-standing and most successful of Trent Valley gravel companies. Up to the mid-1960s, owing to the relatively low manpower requirement of the industry as a whole, and the specialised nature of many jobs, most of the employees of Trent Gravels had been internally trained. At operative level, this was carried out on the basis of new starters working closely with an experienced operator until judged by the foreman to be sufficiently competent to work unsupervised. Managers were free to participate in the recently implemented national training schemes; the company had no planned training policy of its own at that time. Perhaps more worryingly for the company, the lack of formal induction procedures for new employees appeared to lead directly to a high labour wastage rate, with relatively high numbers of operatives leaving within four years of commencement. In order to combat this, and to raise general levels of job and product knowledge, short induction sessions were implemented, to be followed by in-house training.

Most former gravel workers interviewed agreed that the majority of their training, in the early days at least, consisted of learning on the job from more experienced hands. At some quarries the process was semi-formal, with a reasonably logical progression leading from competence in one area to introduction to another. At others, the initiative was taken by individual employees themselves, with, for example, general operatives wanting to learn how to drive the excavators, typically the most coveted job in the quarry. Bryan Atkin remembers his early days at Acton Quarry after deciding to leave school during the sixth form:

> I would go down to the quarry and ride shotgun with the tipper drivers which led to getting an interview for William Cooper & Sons and they set me on as conveyor attendant. I was on the conveyors for a few months and then I helped look after the crusher and then went all through the plant. In those days one of the fundamental differences was that most people started at the bottom and looked on it as a career, a career as a 'quarry op'. You started at the bottom and you did every job but nobody talked about 'team-building' because it was naturally part of it. You were taken under someone else's wing; it was a family.

This 'system' was relatively informal and far from perfect – 'you would learn the hard way, they were cruel to be kind' – but had the benefit of building camaraderie. The larger companies relied on more formal procedures. Nigel Hunt started work as an apprentice mobile plant fitter at Hoveringham Gravels at the age of fifteen, in 1968. He still has his copy of the indenture to prove the fact, as well as the contract he signed when appointed foreman at the age of twenty-three, which set out his responsibilities under the Mines and Quarries Act. Both documents are enclosed in a folder embossed with the words 'Welcome to Hoveringham'.

Over the years, more formal induction procedures have become general across the industry, largely in response to the implementation of increasingly rigorous health and safety regulations. At Attenborough Quarry new starters are now given a full training package which includes basic health and safety matters and environmental issues, and spend two days under the close supervision of the AQM before being trained for a specific job according to requirements. After six months they are assessed according to NVQ standards and, if necessary, receive more training in advance of reassessment. Training courses specific to particular jobs, such as welding skills for fitters, and excavator driving, have been in existence for some years. In pre-hydraulic days, the training course for excavator drivers would take six months and consisted of a mix of college-based knowledge acquisition, on-site application and, in some cases, intensive training at the machine manufacturer's works. Some workers come into the industry already trained for their main job, such as those who have completed mechanical plant fitter's apprenticeships in another industry.

With regard to the training of employees in the range of skills necessary to make the step up towards management, the most successful innovation of the post-war period has been the Doncaster Assisted Private Study (DAPS) course, which has been running since the early 1970s. Based on the principle of taking students away from the workplace for a few hours each week, the course prepares candidates for the Institute of Quarrying's Professional Examination, which is at a level equivalent to Higher National Certificate. Following its launch in 1971, senior figures in the industry started to see the course as a way of testing the 'stamina' of potential managers. Generally speaking the course, which transferred to the University of Derby in 2007, has been popular with both employers and workers. According to Bryan Atkin:

> It was brilliant because the people on the course were of a similar standard and it dealt with quarrying: quarrying ops, quarrying engineering, health and safety, and management in *real* terms – how to make money, the right motors and so on, things that actually meant something to people who had to operate a quarry.

While the move towards more formal training has been broadly welcomed by the industry, there is also a recognition that qualifications are not for everyone and there is still a place within sand and gravel quarrying for people with other attributes. Gary Pell, who is in charge of induction and training at Attenborough Quarry, still feels there is room for people who bring more traditional qualities to the job:

> People tend to come into this industry who have perhaps not had the education to get an apprenticeship or whatever, and the introduction of salaries has boosted the morale of the men and made people feel they have a skill, something to offer. But there's still room for people like [the man] who is camped out on top of the bins and pushes buttons to make material go in one bin or another. It's not a job that you or I would do and it could be done automatically; we've compared his salary with the cost of installing and maintaining a camera system, but realistically you have to have a man up there who is watching the whole time. But he loves it up there! It's his world, it's him 50 foot up in the air on his *Jack Jones*, out of the way. He's got a sense of humour, a kettle, a seat, and his panel – that's it! But you've got to have these guys because you're not going to have someone with a degree sitting up there.

Managers and management styles

It is often said within the industry that under the 1954 Mines and Quarries Act quarry managers were given the same degree of control, and relative lack of outside scrutiny, as the captain of a ship. It is also clear from the tone of articles in *The Quarry Manager's Journal*, founded as early as 1918, that in aspirational terms the typical quarry manager saw himself as a practical version of the bank manager, an authority figure worthy of deference. Yet within the Trent Valley gravel industry, at least, the majority of quarry owners and managers enjoyed good relations with their workforce and, in some cases, earned their affection. This was often in spite of a clearly defined hierarchy, particularly evident in the 1950s. The most prominent quarry owner in the Trent Valley was Harold Needler of Hoveringham Gravels. Dorothy Winn, who ran the office at Hoveringham, often carried out the additional duties of his unofficial personal assistant:

> Harold Needler used to come down about once a week. He would ring up to say he was coming and I would have to get one of the lorry drivers – if they were going into town or into Southwell – to get some smoked salmon. Then I would have to cook it for his lunch on this little grill in the office. Occasionally his wife would come with him with their children, Christopher and Stephanie, and I would have Stephanie on my desk in a carry-cot while Mrs Needler went shopping in Nottingham. Christopher would have been about five then, and if Mr Needler took him down to the quarry I would have the job of cleaning him up again before he went home.

When she worked in the Hoveringham canteen during the 1970s Angela Hunt would occasionally meet the chairman, as well as his son and successor, when they attended board meetings: 'He was a very friendly man, Christopher too. Christopher Needler used to come to work in an E-type Jaguar; Harold Needler had a Rolls Royce with a personalised number plate.' James Marston Spurrier, squire of Marston-on-Dove and owner of Hilton Quarry, was another highly visible proprietor. According to former employee Terry Cliff:

> Mr Spurrier was quite popular, but you would be expected to call him 'sir'. When I helped with beating at the shoots, members of the aristocracy such as Lord Scarsdale would be there, and this was the social *milieu* of the Spurriers; he was also chairman of the local magistrates. He would be out and about every day in his trademark green Rover 14, always with his little black-and-tan dachshund with him. Sometimes he would say that the car made him too visible – the men knew when he was coming!

Among the managers, those who are remembered with greatest affection are the ones who gained the respect of their workers. In the opinion of Barry Hulland:

> There wasn't a feeling of 'them and us' between management and workers. It was more inclusive, mainly because managers had come up through the ranks. At social functions you'd find directors sitting at the table with all us lads and I don't think you'd get that now. Some of them were good old characters.

This was in the days before the concerted policy of turning quarry management into a graduate profession and many, if not most, managers had reached that position from jobs in the industry at a lower level. Bryan Atkin recalls that at Acton:

> In the 1970s and 80s the people who were above the manager, and possibly above them, had also worked in the quarry at some stage, like Keith Andrews [who] started as a conveyor attendant and his father had been a conveyor attendant before him, and that doesn't happen much any more. The managers then would be sort of the equivalent of a foreman now, not too much paperwork. On site only basic paperwork was done, the other stuff was done elsewhere.

The mid-1960s saw the introduction of 'management science' to the organisation of quarrying operations and by the end of the decade there were calls from many in the industry to move towards graduate recruitment. They were answered most enthusiastically by the larger companies which, by the start of the 1970s, were taking on new managers with degrees in subjects such as civil and mining engineering, and geology. For those gravel men who had grown up under a system where workers became foremen and, eventually, managers themselves, the change was not always entirely welcome. Deg Bellamy was foreman at Girton when, on one occasion, one of the company's new managers came to check on operations:

> There's a big difference between people with experience and those managers who have learned it out of a book. One of the top managers came along just as about eight boats had pulled up. 'That's no good,' he said, 'You want one coming every hour'. But he had no idea what he was talking about. I said: 'It's a tidal river – they can only come with the tide!'

Tom Dodsley, who subsequently rose to the position of Area Manager, entered the ranks at Hoveringham before the move towards graduate recruitment was fully underway and would have some sympathy with this situation:

> Graduate managers are not expected to be hands-on with the day-to-day running of the plant. When I first started, someone said you really want to listen to the plant, and I wondered what it meant. It's the fact that problems can be discerned from a change in sound, and I can still point out problems to managers when I arrive on site. There have been big changes in the nature of the relationship between management and workers. Managers would say what was going to be done and it was done – nobody would question the boss. Those days are long gone; the guys at the sharp end have often got more knowledge than people in managerial positions.

While others would share this view of the need for managers and men to meet on equal terms, they would not necessarily have such positive recollections of the style of management prevalent in the 1970s. Mick Turner became manager at Attenborough in 1994:

> They needed to see me as part of the team and not just the gaffer. Years ago you would doff your cap at the quarry manager, and that was the same from the

1920s right down to the 80s and 90s because under section 98 of the old Quarries Act he was a *demi-god*. A lot of the managers saw themselves like that. The only management training we did twenty years ago was 'discipline and dismissal' which always struck me as odd – why not do 'recruitment and selection' first? Because if you do that right you don't have to do the other! But we always devoted a lot of time to how to sack people.

Perhaps the most striking difference between the old-style quarry managers and the new is that it is now accepted that the position has an explicit public dimension. The inexorable rise of environmental issues up the public agenda has meant that managers are required to play the role of community liaison officers on behalf of their employers. Inevitably, this has meant that communication and interpersonal skills are becoming as highly valued in potential managers as specific knowledge of quarrying processes. For Mick Turner, this change reflects a shift in the entire relationship between quarries and communities:

> The selection process, from the quarry operative to the general manager, is massively different from how it was. It used to be based on family relationships, and men would take turns at being foreman irrespective of suitability for the job. As managers over the last fifteen years we have had a lot more training in human relations, customer relations, and in partnerships with local residents. The difference between the Mines and Quarries Acts of 1954 and 1999 is the extent of the change in working culture.

Social life and job satisfaction

The relatively small scale and transient nature of gravel working has meant that the social networks that were a particularly noticeable feature of the coal industry, in particular, in the 20th century, have not developed. By and large, even when workers came from the same village, the end of the working day meant the end of social contact. No doubt this was in part due to the long hours that many workers were putting in, sometimes, as we have seen, in combination with agricultural work.

A notable exception was provided by Hoveringham Gravels, which deliberately fostered a highly visible local presence with its 'Mammoth' buses bringing workers in each day from the surrounding villages. Less obtrusively, the company also provided a meals-on-wheels service for the local elderly, according to canteen worker Angela Hunt 'by way of putting something back into the community'. Hoveringham also did much to foster the well-being of its employees. Angela has fond memories of a busy social life facilitated by the company:

> There was a summer disco, often at Calverton Lido, and a Christmas Dinner Dance that was paid for. They had a football team in which my brother played, and I played in the ladies' hockey team on Sundays. We played in orange and black and were called the 'Honey Bees'. We would have bus trips to, say, a Sheffield

venue to see pop concerts – they would put a trip on the notice board and people would sign up. They did look after the workforce; the company took pride in their workers.

The problem with playing football for a gravel company, however, was that when Hoveringham extended its quarry the team temporarily lost its pitch. But there was always something to do at weekends, as Tom Dodsley recalls: 'There would be trips to the seaside – two coaches going to Blackpool on a Saturday morning and coming back Sunday – then there was Hoveringham Social Club, and a cricket team; it was really good stuff.' Deg Bellamy also remembers Hoveringham as an employer which took an active interest in the social life of its workers (Fig 95):

They would always have a Christmas party and would take us to Nottingham, with our wives. A couple of times a year they would put £15 towards drinks and a meal at a local pub, and they had a box at Nottingham Forest [Football Club] and anyone who had been there fifteen years could have a ticket.

Other companies were not to be outdone, however. Barry Hulland remembers the situation changing for the better when the quarries at which he worked were taken over by Blue Circle Aggregates in the mid-1960s:

Every Christmas there were three functions, one of which was totally free and the other two were subsidised. They were a very good company to work for, good salary, everything. I would go to about three Institute of Quarrying Dinner Dances a year and you'd see people from the other quarries.

The same company took over Hilton Gravel, Terry Cliff's employer:

Another improvement was that they had two full-time welfare officers and they would set targets for the quarries to run accident-free. If you achieved this over a number of years you would have an evening with a meal and free bar at a hotel. The top man of Blue Circle would come up from HQ at Portland House in London and he would circulate among the men which made a very favourable impression.

They started a fishing club, a cricket team, walking club, swimming and sailing clubs at Manor Park, King's Bromley, which was a former gravel quarry; my wife and I used to take the lads sailing at weekends. And there was a swimming club that was run from the Hilton offices and we would go to Burton baths.

Many former workers in the sand and gravel industry reflect on their days in quarrying with affection and pride. In some cases this is a recognition of the sense of belonging that came from being part of a particular firm, such as the former Hoveringham employees who note that the company made presentations for loyal service after just five years, not twenty-five as was the norm; or the RMC drivers who took pride in wearing the company uniform and tie. In others it was the camaraderie, being part of a team, out in all weathers but knowing where each workmate kept their kettle for a warming brew. One current worker talks excitedly of the continuous nature of the job, the sense that there is always something happening, new places to dig, boats to fill with gravel.

Managers talk of their pride in the quarries for which they were responsible: workers kept busy and happy, production flowing, the site clean and tidy, a reasonably tolerated element in the local community. More than one former worker talks of their surprise that they ended up staying in the industry for years, often a working lifetime. Terry Cliff looks back at a largely fulfilling working life, first with Hilton Gravel and then its successor, Blue Circle. He remembers how, as a young boy playing in a worked-out part of Hilton gravel pit, and being chased away by an ex-army foreman with a shotgun, he vowed he would never work there when he was older. In the event, as a gravel lorry driver, much of his life was closely tied to the fortunes of that same pit. Barry Hulland worked mainly at another Derbyshire quarry, Repton, and knew Terry well. He probably sums up the lasting feelings of many Trent Valley gravel workers:

It was fun. Every job is what you make it – I enjoyed my time, it was good, I can't say it wasn't. You can't work all that time in one job if you don't like it. Can you?

Interviewees

1. Michael Arthur, MBE (b. 1939). Technical Assistant then Assistant Manager and Training Officer for Trent Gravels at Attenborough; inaugurator of DAPS course, Doncaster College, from 1971; Technical Director of the Institute of Quarrying from 1984 until retirement in 1999.

Michael Arthur

2. Bryan Atkin (b. 1950). Started as a conveyor attendant before becoming Quarry Manager at Acton and subsequently Rugeley; spent two years as a quarry manager in Cheshire and North Wales for Tarmac; since redundancy from RMC in 2004 works as HGV driver delivering aggregates.

Bryan Atkin

3. Ken Bagnall (b. 1938). Former excavator driver at Acton Quarry.

4. Derrick 'Deg' Bellamy (b. 1929). Former excavator driver, fitter and foreman at Besthorpe and Girton quarries.

Deg Bellamy

5. Mick Bugg (b. 1944). Boatman at Attenborough Quarry following career in the RN submarine fleet and HM prison service.

Mick Bugg

6. G Campbell. Former owner of Gunthorpe Quarry.

7. Terry Cliff (b. 1934). Former lorry driver, Hilton Gravel.

Terry Cliff

8. Tom Dodsley (b. 1948). Started as Trainee Quarry Superintendent at Hoveringham Gravels' Holme Pierrepont Quarry in 1971; Operations Manager, Tarmac East Midlands until retirement in 2007.

Tom Dodsley

9. Keith Farrell (b. 1956). Excavator driver at Acton, now at a quarry in Shropshire.

10. Barry Hulland (b. 1946). Former HGV driver with Midland Gravel Co and Deputy Manager for Blue Circle Aggregates, Hemington.

Barry Hulland

11. Angela Hunt (b. 1955). Former canteen worker at Hoveringham Quarry.

12. Nigel Hunt (b. 1953). Former mobile plant fitter, Hoveringham Gravels Ltd.

Nigel Hunt

13. Gary Pell (b. 1959). Assistant Quarry Manager, Attenborough Quarry.

Gary Pell

14. Dennis Thacker (b. 1939). Former dumper and excavator driver at Besthorpe and Girton Quarries.
15. Jack Thornhill (b. 1933). Former excavator driver at Winthorpe Quarry.
16. John 'Durgin' Thornhill (b. 1914). Started life on Trent barges at age of twelve; helped open Winthorpe Quarry in 1939 and, following naval service in Malta during WWII, was foreman at Besthorpe and Girton.

Left to right: Jack Thornhill, Dennis Thacker, Durgin Thornhill

17. Mick Turner (b. 1954). Sand and Aggregates Area Manager, Cemex, based at Attenborough Quarry.

Mick Turner

18. Dorothy Winn (née Scrivener, b. 1930). Former office supervisor at Hoveringham Quarry.

Dorothy Winn

19. Bob Woodbridge (b. 1948). Senior Area Geologist, Hanson Aggregates.

Bob Woodbridge

Gazetteer of principal sites, with dates of first verifiable working

Derbyshire

Aston-upon-Trent	1589
Barrow-upon-Trent	1939
Drakelow	1950
Draycott	1948
Egginton	1936
Elvaston	1968
Hilton	1924
Melbourne	1908
Repton	1936
Sawley	1948
Shardlow	1709
Stenson	1936
Swadlincote	1928
Swarkestone	1928
Weston-upon-Trent	1709
Willington	1940
Wilne	1709

Leicestershire

Hemington	1947

Lincolnshire

Burton Fen	1933
North Hykeham	1946
Messingham	1937
Whisby	1933

Nottinghamshire

Attenborough	1930
Beeston	1876
Besthorpe	1939
Bleasby	1947
Bramcote	1928
Carlton-on-Trent	1922
Collingham	1940
Colwick	1928
Crankley Point	1940
Cromwell	1940
Dunkirk	1940
Farndon	1885
Girton	1950
Gunthorpe	1948
Holme	1939
Holme Pierrepont	1954
Hoveringham	1939
Langford Lowfields	1990
Lockington	1951
Newark	1912
New Balderton	1932
Rolleston	1854
South Muskham	1875
Sutton-on-Trent	1912
Winthorpe	1939

Staffordshire

Acton (Whitmore)	1801
Alrewas	1800
Barton-under-Needwood	1963
Branston	1932
Fenton	1896
Kings Bromley	1940
Longton	1932
Meir	1817
Normacot	1725
Oulton	1912
Rugeley	1876
Stone	1912
Stretton	1924
Trentham	1770

Gazetteer of significant independent operators and main quarries, with earliest verified date of operation in the Trent Valley region

Acme Gravels (Nottingham) Ltd, Beeston	1941
Apex Sand & Gravel Ltd, North Hykeham	1946
Branston Gravels Ltd	1932
Burton & Branston Gravel Co Ltd	1940
Butterley Aggregates Ltd	1949
Central Sand & Gravel Co, Normacot	1940
Coolee Ltd, Bramcote	1928
G M Campbell Quarries Ltd, Gunthorpe	1963
T C Campbell Ltd, Gunthorpe	1958
William Cooper & Sons, Acton	1966
Derbyshire Gravel & Aggregates Ltd, Swarkestone	1936
Drakelow Gravel Co	1960
Finningley Gravel Co Ltd, Whisby	1937
Gravel Sales (Repton) Ltd	1952
Gunthorpe Gravels (Trent) Ltd	1948
Hartsholme Gravel & Sand Co Ltd	1946
Benjamin Hilton, Normacot	1881
William Hilton, Normacot	1924
Hilton Gravel Ltd	1924
Hoveringham Gravel Co Ltd	1939
Hoveringham Gravels Ltd	1947
CAEC Howard, North Hykeham	1946
Inns & Co Ltd, Besthorpe	1941
Lightwood Concrete Aggregates Ltd, Normacot	1928

Lincoln & Hull Water Transport Ltd, Winthorpe	1939
Lincoln Sand & Gravel Co Ltd, Burton Fen	1933
Meir Road Sand & Gravel Pits, Normacot	1932
Midland Gravel Co Ltd	1934
Mugginton Sand and Gravel Co Ltd	1950
Naybro Stone Co Ltd, Acton	1940
Newark Gravel & Concrete Co Ltd, New Balderton	1932
Pontylue Sand & Ballast, Hemington, Shardlow	1986
Repton Sand and Gravel Co Ltd	1950
J Rhead, Fenton (Stoke)	1896
Norman S Rhead, Longton	1932
Sawley Kastone Co Ltd, Sawley	1948
Searancke, Edwin J, Swadlincote	1928
Star Gravels, Besthorpe	1950
Stenson Gravel Co, Stenson	1936
Swarkestone Sand & Gravels Ltd, Swarkestone	1928
Robert Teal Ltd, Whisby	1922
Tower Quarries Ltd, Whisby	1933
Trent Concrete Ltd, Colwick	1928
Trent Gravels Ltd, Attenborough	1929
Trentham Gravel Co Ltd	1932
J Wardle & Co, Longton	1936
J Whitfield & Son, Normacot	1982
Willington Gravels Ltd, Egginton	1936

Planning conditions for an extension to Hoveringham Quarry, 1947

1. Topsoil and subsoil to be removed a reasonable distance in advance of excavation for sand and gravel and to be stocked in a suitable position on the site for reuse in forming or covering the batter [slope] to the banks.
2. Where land bounding the land which is the subject of this application is to be retained in agricultural use, excavation for sand and gravel shall be finished with a batter of 2 to 1 from the boundary inwards.
3. All islands which may be left in the excavation are to be levelled off as directed.
4. All necessary action to be taken to prevent nuisance and damage by growth of weeds whether within the workings or on stocks of soil.
5. Land to remain in agricultural use until actually required for mineral workings.
6. So far as practicable existing trees and hedges to be preserved.
7. Rivers, streams and natural drainage channels to be reinstated to appropriate levels to ensure their functioning in a satisfactory manner.
8. The winning of surface minerals shall not proceed nearer than 15 feet from existing public highways, bridle or accommodation roads.
9. Before finally vacating the site one month's notice to be given to the Planning Authority and the whole site to be left clean and tidy and all plant, machinery and buildings removed unless otherwise agreed that certain buildings may remain.

(Nottinghamshire Archives, DC SW/4/8/32/1)

Places to visit

Attenborough Nature Reserve & Visitor Centre
Barton Lane
Attenborough
Beeston
Nottingham NG9 6DY
http://www.attenboroughnaturecentre.co.uk/

National Stone Centre
Porter Lane
Middleton
Wirksworth
Derbyshire DE4 4L
http://www.nationalstonecentre.org.uk/

Bibliography

Primary sources
National Archives

Crown Estate

CRES 58/
1365 SAGA code of practice, 1968–81
1545 Annual returns of extraction of sand and gravel, 1966–72

Dept of Scientific and Industrial Research

DSIR 4/
3867 SAGA Technical Cttee, notes of meetings, papers and related correspondence, 1977–82

Dept of Economic Affairs

EW 8/
426 Sand and gravel, 1966–69

Ministry of Housing and Local Government

HLG 89/
6 Proposed Advisory Cttee on Sand and Gravel, 1947–48
84 Advisory Cttee on Sand & Gravel [Waters Cttee]: general evidence from outside bodies, 1946–53
85 Waters: agenda minutes, 1946–48
101 Waters Cttee: discussion of reports with LPAs etc, 1948–50
102 Waters Cttee: general procedure, 1949–52
225 Waters Cttee: filling materials, 1949–54
262 Waters Cttee: establishment and constitution, 1945–54
263 Waters Cttee: agenda and minutes, 1948–54
264 Waters Cttee: reports, parts I & II, 1947–49
266 Waters Cttee: general procedure and programme of work, 1946–54
267 Waters Cttee: discussion of report parts I & II with LPAs, 1950–56
269 Waters Cttee: discussion with LPAs re Trent Valley, 1949–57
538–40 Preparation of map showing sand and gravel pits in Great Britain, 1952–69
542 Sand and gravel production: estimates of future demand, 1957–68
546 Waters Cttee: report 1952, first review, 1958–64
573–4 Sand and gravel production survey: review of gravel Cttee reports, 1957–65
585 Waters Report: after-treatment of disused workings, 1957–61
586 Advisory Committee on Sand and Gravel, 1971

89 Advisory Cttee on Sand & Gravel [Waters] Report: first review, technical data by geological research section, 1956–72

96 Waters Report: data for inclusion in part 13 of report, 1947–52

97 Waters Report: proposed fund for treatment of worked pits, 1956–64

98 Trent Valley Sand & Gravel Review [TVGR]: technical data by geological research, 1955–72

99 TVGR: co-ordination of gravel extraction and waste disposal, 1948–64

00 TVGR: Waters recommendations, 1958–61

12–13 Trent Valley: Waters Report, first review, 1948

72 City of Nottingham: Waters Report, implementation, 1950–53

90 TVGR: Waters recommendations, 1961–66

024 Transport of sand and gravel freight by rail, 1963–67

066 Minister's discussions with SAGA, 1965–66

108 Ministry of Public Buildings & Works: working party on aggregates in the construction industry: alternatives to sand and gravel, 1966–69

175 Sand and gravel reviews: policy, programme, 1968–71

184–6 Staffordshire Development Plan: review of sand and gravel requirements, 1968–74

HLG 129/

69 Repton RDC: Salterford Bridge, Egginton, appeal against refusal of permission to reclaim sand and gravel workings with iron waste, 1971–73

Dept of Labour and Employment

LAB 18/

001 Ceramics, Glass & Mineral Products Industry Training Board: consultation with SAGA, 1964–66

694 SAGA: note of meeting with the department's Training Division; future of levy/grant and the status of the proposed National Training Agency, 1972

LAB 83/

6–7 SAGA, 1941–74

60 Sand and gravel, East Midlands, 1939–40

Ministry of Agriculture, Fisheries and Food

MAF 107/

33 Sand and gravel: plans and returns, 1951–52

34 Sand and gravel: plans, 1943–55

MAF 141/

55–6 Sand and gravel sites: Trent Valley, 1947–56

12 Restoration of worked out sand and gravel pits: proposals to charge a levy to finance an after-treatment fund, 1948–60

74 Exchanges of information between Ministry and SAGA, 1955–66

342 Sand and gravel sites, Trent Valley: agricultural implications, 1958–65

482 Liaison arrangements with SAGA, 1961–70

Ministry of Power

POWE 26/

661 Sand and Gravel Quarries (Overhanging) (Exemption) Regulations, 1958

Ministry of Works: Ancient Monuments Boards & Inspectorate

WORK 14/

2980 Mineral working (sand and gravel): risk to archaeological sites, liaison with local authorities, 1959–69

WORK 45/

204 Sand and gravel haulage rates, 1946–49

205 Waters Cttee: committee papers, 1946–48

206 Waters Cttee: estimates of future requirements, 1946–59

207 Sand and gravel: reclamation of pits, 1946–61

254 Review of sand and gravel reserves: Trent Valley, 1959–66

256 Review of sand and gravel reserves: replacements for sand and gravel in concrete, 1960–67

280 Review of sand and gravel reserves: policy, 1961–70

294 Land and natural resources: planning mineral extraction inc sand and gravel, policy and procedure 1958–64

451 Sand and gravel: data for proposed review of reserves in 1970, 1967–69

494 Sand and gravel: substitute materials for concrete manufacture, 1968–71

501 Land and resources planning: mineral extraction industries inc sand and gravel, policy and procedure for approving development plans, 1969–71

532 Early warning and constant watch system: pricing policy, sand and gravel; attempts to establish the cost of transport, 1968–70

622 Department of Economic Affairs, working party prices and incomes: investigation of the non-statutory early warning system for sand and gravel; correspondence with the DoE and SAGA, 1969–70

Leicester, Leicestershire and Rutland Record Office

DE 3736 Photographs, inc gravel workings

DE 5185/14–17 Leicestershire Minerals Plans; Sand and Gravel Workings, 1945–63

Lincolnshire Archives

2 AMC 4A/8/8 Invoice from Lincs Sand & Gravel Co to Mrs Amcotts of Kettlethorpe Hall, 1936

2 AMC 4B/3/1–3 Board of Trade to Mrs Amcotts, 1908

2 AMC 4B/4/1–7 Trent Navigation Co to Mrs Amcotts, 1911, 1921

Nottinghamshire Archives

DC SW/4/8/32/1 Plans and planning consent for gravel working by Hoveringham Gravels Ltd Hoveringham 1947

DD H/151/104–7 Correspondence re gravel working at Farndon, 1900–02

DD H/152/156 Payments for gravel at South Muskham

DD H/161/399–400 Surveys of Manners Sutton land on island in river excavated for gravel by Commissioner of Foston Bridge road, 1854–55

DD H/161/401 Permits from Manners Sutton agents to Martin Starbuck allowing removal of a boat-load of gravel from the Trent at Rolleston, 1877–1881

DD NM/22/3/32 Public meeting at Coddington re gravel extraction for A46 relief road, 1986–88

DD SY/90a Damage done to properties at Thrumpton and Sawley by gravel extraction from Trent, 1838

R 8055(j) Parish notebook of Revd Abraham Youle of West Retford, 1807

Staffordshire Record Office

593/N/2/2/3/12–13 Trentham Gravel Pits – Cash Books, 1887–1919
593/B/1/11/18 Lease of a gravel quarry at Meir, 1817
593/B/1/20/6 Gravel pits on Normacot Common
603/N/3/11 Records of the Paget Family c 1810–18
615/M/1/6 Map of land near Bearshay, Alrewas nd c 1800
1057 /J/36/1–4 Correspondence re gravel at Burton 18th–19th C
(W)1743/10 Plan of a gravel pit at Acton belonging to Edward Mainwaring Esq, 1801
Staffordshire CC Development Plan, 1951

Private Collections

Michael Arthur

Trent Gravels Ltd; Attenborough Quarry & Nature Reserve; History of Ready-Mixed Concrete Industry

Cemex, Attenborough

Trent Gravels Ltd

Nigel Hunt

Hoveringham Gravels Ltd

Directories

British Telecom, Midland Industrial & Commercial Directory, 1982
British Telecom Business Pages, East Midlands: 1986–93
Derby County Borough Directory, 1952–57
Directory of Quarries, 2005
Kelly's Directory of Derbys, 1908–57
Kelly's Directory of Leics, 1941–66
Kelly's Directory of Lincs, 1933–75
Kelly's Directory of Notts, 1881–1956
Kelly's Directory of Staffs, 1896–1940
Long Eaton Official Handbook, 1936–48
Post Office Directory of Derby, Leicester, Rutland and Nottinghamshire, 1876
Post Office Directory of Staffs, 1876
Shardlow RDC Official Guide, 1936–41
White's Directory of Notts, 1885–1914

Secondary sources: books

Bridgland, D R, Howard, A J, White, M J & White T S, 2006 *The Trent Valley: Archaeology and Landscap* *of the Ice Age.* Durham University

Edwards, K C, 1966 *Nottingham and its Region.* Nottingham: British Association for the Advancement Science

Farey, J, 1811–17 *General View of the Agriculture and Minerals of Derbyshire*, 3 vols. London

Greenslade, M J & Jenkins, J G, 1967 *Victoria County History of Staffordshire vol II.* Oxford: Institute Historical Research and Oxford University Press

Ingram, J H, 1955 *The River Trent.* London: Cassell

Littler, A, 2000 *Sand and Gravel Production.* Nottingham: Institute of Quarrying

Knight, D & Howard, A J, 2004 *Trent Valley Landscapes.* King's Lynn: Heritage Marketing and Publication:

Knight, D & Vyner B, 2006 *Making Archaeology Matter: Quarrying and Archaeology in the Trent Valley.* Yo Archaeological Trust

SAGA (Sand and Gravel Association of Great Britain), 1967 *Pit and Quarry Textbook.* London: MacDonald

Stanier, P, 1995 *Quarries of England and Wales.* Truro: Twelveheads

Stanier, P, 2000 *Stone Quarry Landscapes: The Archaeology of Quarrying in England.* Stroud: Tempus

Stanier, P, 2000 *Quarries and Quarrying.* Princes Risborough: Shire

Stone, R, 2005 *The River Trent.* Chichester: Phillimore

Taylor, M, 2000 *The River Trent Navigation.* Stroud: Tempus

Tringham, N J, 2003 *Victoria County History of Staffordshire vol IX, Burton upon Trent.* Woodbridge: Institu of Historical Research and Boydell & Brewer

Weir, C, 1991 *The Nottinghamshire Heritage.* Chichester: Phillimore

Secondary sources: journals

Cement, Lime and Gravel

The Quarry Managers' Journal

Quarry Management and Products

Secondary sources: articles

Thomas, TA, 1999 'Tarmac's Derbyshire Heritage', *Tarmac Papers* 1999

Reports

Bradley, A, Buchli, V, Fairclough, G, Hicks, D, Miller J & Schofield, J, 2004 *Change and Creation: Histor Landscape Character 1950–2000.* London: English Heritage

British Geological Survey, 2005 *Construction Aggregates*, Mineral Planning Factsheet

British Geological Survey, May 2007 *Collation of the results of the 2005 Aggregate Minerals Survey fo England and Wales* (available from http://www.communities.gov.uk/publications/planningandbuildin aggregatesmineralssurvey2005)

Brown, T J, & Highley, D E, 2006 *Primary Aggregate Reserves in England 1990–2004.* British Geologica Survey Report CR/06/168. Nottingham: Keyworth

Colman, T B & Cooper, D C, 2000 *Exploration for Metalliferous and Related Minerals in Britain: A Guide.* British Geological Survey, DTI Minerals Programme Publication No. 1, 2nd edn (available from http://www.bgs.ac.uk/mineralsuk/free_downloads/home.html)

Derbyshire County Council, November 2002 *Derby and Derbyshire Minerals Local Plan, Adopted Edition, April 2000: Incorporating First Alteration: Chapter 13 – Coal*

East Midlands Aggregates Working Party, 2006 *Survey and Annual Report for Calendar Year 2004*

Hetherington, L E, Brown, T J, Lusty, P A J, Hitchen, K & Colman, T B, 2007 *British Geological Survey United Kingdom Minerals Yearbook 2006; Statistical data to 2005.* Nottingham: Keyworth

Nottinghamshire County Council, *Nottinghamshire Minerals Local Plan, Revised Deposit May 2003*

Quarry Products Association, 2005 *Sustainable Development – Building our Strategy* (available from www.qpa.org/downloads/sust_devA4.pdf)

Quarry Products Association, 2007 *Sustainable Development Report 2007* (available from http://www.qpa.org/sus_report01.htm)

Staffordshire County Council, *Staffordshire and Stoke-on-Trent Minerals Local Plan 1994–2006* (available from: http://www.staffordshire.gov.uk/environment/developmentcontrol/planning/policy/mineralsPlanningPolicy/mineralsLocalPlan.htm)

Central government reports and publications

Minerals Planning Guidance 1: General Considerations and the Development Plan System

Minerals Planning Guidance 2: Applications, Permissions and Conditions

Minerals Planning Guidance 4: The Review of Mineral Working Sites

Minerals Planning Guidance 7: The Reclamation of Mineral Workings

Minerals Planning Guidance 10: Provision of Raw Material for the Cement Industry

Minerals Planning Guidance 14: Environment Act 1995 – Review of Mineral Planning Permissions

Minerals Policy Statement 1: Planning and Minerals

Minerals Policy Statement 2: Controlling and Mitigating the Environmental Effects of Minerals Extraction in England

Planning Policy Guidance 2: Green Belts

Planning Policy Guidance 7: The Countryside – Environmental Quality and Economic and Social Development

Planning Policy Guidance 9: Nature Conservation

Planning Policy Guidance 15: Planning and the Historic Environment

Planning Policy Guidance 16: Archaeology and Planning

Planning Policy Guidance 23: Planning and Pollution Control

Planning Policy Statement 1: Delivering Sustainable Development

Planning Policy Statement 9: Biodiversity and Geological Conservation

Regional Planning Guidance 8: Regional Planning Guidance for the East Midlands

Index

Entries in bold refer to the illustrations